S0-ANX-370

URBANIZATION
IN THE COMMONWEALTH
CARIBBEAN

Westview Special Studies

The concept of Westview Special Studies is a response to the continuing crisis in academic and informational publishing. Library budgets are being diverted from the purchase of books and used for data banks, computers, micromedia, and other methods of information retrieval. Interlibrary loan structures further reduce the edition sizes required to satisfy the needs of the scholarly community. Economic pressures on university presses and the few private scholarly publishing companies have greatly limited the capacity of the industry to properly serve the academic and research communities. As a result, many manuscripts dealing with important subjects, often representing the highest level of scholarship, are no longer economically viable publishing projects—or, if accepted for publication, are typically subject to lead times ranging from one to three years.

Westview Special Studies are our practical solution to the problem. As always, the selection criteria include the importance of the subject, the work's contribution to scholarship, and its insight, originality of thought, and excellence of exposition. We accept manuscripts in camera-ready form, typed, set, or word processed according to specifications laid out in our comprehensive manual, which contains straightforward instructions and sample pages. The responsibility for editing and proofreading lies with the author or sponsoring institution, but our editorial staff is always available to answer questions and provide guidance.

The result is a book printed on acid-free paper and bound in sturdy library-quality soft covers. We manufacture these books ourselves using equipment that does not require a lengthy make-ready process and that allows us to publish first editions of 500 to 1,500 copies and to reprint even smaller quantities as needed. Thus, we can produce Special Studies quickly and can keep even very specialized books in print as long as there is a demand for them.

About the Book and Author

Focusing on Barbados, Trinidad and Tobago, Jamaica, and Guyana, Professor Hope examines the determinants and socioeconomic consequences associated with urban population growth. He documents demographic trends in the region, examines government policies that inadvertently encourage urbanization, and discusses the effects of too-rapid growth on urban services and the employment rate. He concludes with policy suggestions for managing growth, counteracting the urban bias, and stemming rural-to-urban migration. Throughout the book, the author uses a multidisciplinary approach that draws on economics, sociology, demography, urban planning, and public administration.

Dr. Kempe Ronald Hope is Fulbright Professor of Economics and Public Policy in the Faculty of Social Sciences and is Visiting Associate Research Fellow in the Institute of Social and Economic Research at the University of the West Indies, Mona Campus, Jamaica. Dr. Hope's previous books include *Guyana: Politics and Development in an Emergent Socialist State* (1985); *The Dynamics of Development and Development Administration* (1984); and *Recent Performance and Trends in the Caribbean Economy* (1980).

TO

DESSETA, DAWN, EUCLYN, AND KEMPE, Jr.

URBANIZATION
IN THE COMMONWEALTH
CARIBBEAN

KEMPE RONALD HOPE

WESTVIEW PRESS / BOULDER AND LONDON

Westview Special Studies on Latin America and the Caribbean

Published in 1986 in the United States of America by Westview Press, Inc.; Frederick A. Praeger, Publisher; 5500 Central Avenue, Boulder, Colorado 80301

Library of Congress Cataloging-in-Publication Data
Hope, Kempe R.
  Urbanization in the Commonwealth Caribbean.
  (Westview special studies on Latin America and
the Caribbean)
  Bibliography: p.
  Includes index.
  1. Cities and towns—Caribbean Area—Growth.
2. Economic development—Caribbean Area. 3. Rural-urban
migration—Caribbean Area. 4. Urban policy—Caribbean
Area. I. Title. II. Series.
HT128.5.A2H66 1986   307.7′6′09729   86-1674
ISBN 0-8133-7182-1

Composition for this book was provided by the author.
This book was produced without formal editing by the publisher.

Printed and bound in the United States of America

6   5   4   3   2   1

CONTENTS

TABLES

PREFACE

The urbanization of the Third World as a result of rapid growth in the urban population has now become a matter of great concern and study by the governments of the Third World nations as well as the international development agencies. Currently, about 75 percent of the world's population live in the Third World and it is projected that by the year 2000 the majority of the world's urban population (66 percent) will reside in the Third World. As the population explosion continues, political and economic pressures will rise enormously in many of those nations. The expulsion of hundreds of thousands of aliens from Nigeria in 1983 and again in 1985 is but one illustration of this point.

Interest in the study of urbanization in the Commonwealth Caribbean has not been intense and, as such, not much in the way of research studies has been produced on the topic *vis-à-vis* the various countries of the region. But urban population growth and its consequences in the Commonwealth Caribbean are critical issues for the future of the region and need more interdisciplinary concern and research endeavours from social scientists, planners, and policy-makers. This book makes one contemporary attempt to synthesize, in a comparative manner, the significance of the trends, consequences, and policy implications of rapid urban population growth and urbanization using, as a case study, Barbados, Guyana, Jamaica, and Trinidad and Tobago — The More Developed Commonwealth Caribbean Countries (MDCC's).

The above four countries chosen for this study are representative of the Commonwealth Caribbean region in terms of social, cultural, and economic structure and they cover a wide geographical area spanning from Guyana in South America through Trinidad and Tobago and Barbados in the Eastern sector (Lesser Antilles) to Jamaica in the Northern sector (Greater Antilles). The Commonwealth Caribbean nations share a history of slavery and British colonialism, some common economic problems as well as some similar socio-economic characteristics. All of the countries lie within the tropics; English is their official language; they are all members of the Caribbean Community (CARICOM); they are all heavily dependent on trade with the United States; and they all suffer from high urban population densities and significant international and internal migration.

This book is divided into five chapters. The first chapter provides an analytical overview of urbanization and economic development in the Third World exploring the various issues with regard to the trends, components, consequences, and management policies. The second chapter begins the Caribbean case study by examining the structure, sources, and the impact of urban population growth and urbanization in the Caribbean. Chapter three provides a discussion of unemployment and labour force participation within the context of urbanization in the Caribbean. Chapter four considers and advocates a set of policies for managing rapid urban population growth and urbanization in the Caribbean, and the final chapter gives a summary and concluding statements on the work.

During the preparation of this book I benefitted from the suggestions and comments of Professor George Roberts of the University of the West Indies, Professor Dennis Rondinelli of Syracuse University, and Dr. Derek Boyd of the University of the West Indies. Needless to say, however, any errors or omissions remain my sole responsibility. I also owe a special debt of gratitude to the graduate students in my public policy courses at the University of the West Indies (on whom the majority of this work was tried out in the form of class lectures and discussions) for their input which provided me with ideas on the improvement of the material as a course text.

Finally, financial support for the completion of this book was provided by the Secretariat for Development Cooperation of the

Organization of American States through research grant BEGES-82506. I gratefully acknowledge that support. However, the opinions expressed are entirely mine and not necessarily those of the OAS.

KEMPE RONALD HOPE

URBANIZATION AND ECONOMIC DEVELOPMENT IN THE THIRD WORLD: AN OVERVIEW

Urbanization is conventionally defined as the process of growth in the urban proportion of a country's entire population, rather than merely in the urban population *per se*. If urbanization is so defined then the appropriate measure of the rate of urbanization is the difference between the growth rates of the urban population and the national population.[1] During the past two decades, there has been rapid urbanization in much of the Third World due primarily to development strategies that emphasized urban growth at the expense of agricultural and rural development. As a result, the rate of increase in the size of the non-agricultural population exceeds the rate of increase in meaningful nonagricultural employment opportunities, thus leading to what has now come to be known as "over-urbanization."

This chapter offers a broad overview of the urbanization dilemma in the Third World - within the context of elusive development - with particular attention to current trends, components, consequences, and policies designed to manage it.

Current Trends in Urbanization

Current urbanization rates in Third World cities are unique in the sense that these trends now result in some global concern. Today, a mere one percent shift of the world's population from rural to urban areas represents 44 million people.[2] Estimates of the United Nations suggest that during the period 1980-2000 there will be a 1.4 billion increase in population in urban centers

Table 1.1

Total Urban Population and Proportion of Population Living in Urban Areas
By Major Areas and Region, 1960-2000
(Millions and Percentages)

REGION/COMPONENT	1960	1970	1980	1990	2000
WORLD TOTAL					
Total Urban	1012.1	1354.4	1806.8	2422.3	3208.0
% Living in Urban Areas	33.9	37.5	41.3	45.9	51.3
LESS DEVELOPED REGIONS					
Total Urban	439.4	651.5	972.4	1453.1	2115.6
% Living in Urban Areas	21.9	25.8	30.5	36.5	43.5
AFRICA					
Total Urban	49.5	80.4	132.9	219.2	345.8
% Living in Urban Areas	18.2	22.9	28.9	35.7	42.5
LATIN AMERICA					
Total Urban	106.6	162.4	240.6	343.3	466.2
% Living in Urban Areas	49.5	57.4	64.7	70.7	75.2
CARIBBEAN					
Total Urban	7.7	11.1	15.7	21.6	28.8
% Living in Urban Areas	38.2	45.1	52.2	58.7	64.6
EAST ASIA					
Total Urban	194.7	265.2	359.5	476.5	622.4
% Living in Urban Areas	24.7	28.6	33.1	38.6	45.4
SOUTH ASIA					
Total Urban	146.9	217.3	329.8	515.7	790.7
% Living in Urban Areas	17.8	20.5	24.0	29.1	36.1
OCEANIA					
Total Urban	10.4	13.7	17.8	22.6	27.1
% Living in Urban Areas	66.2	70.8	75.9	80.4	83.0

SOURCE: United Nations, *Patterns of Urban and Rural Population Growth* (New York: United Nations Population Studies No. 68, 1980).

worldwide (as seen in Table 1.1), of which 1.2 billion will be in the Third World.

By the year 2000, the majority of the world's urban population (66 percent) will reside in the Third World. Between 1950 and 2000, it is anticipated that the urban population of the Third World will grow by a factor of 7.7, or factors of 10.9 in Africa, 6.9 in Latin America, 9.2 in East Asia (excluding Japan), and 7.5 in South Asia. In comparison, the urban population of the more developed regions is expected to grow by a factor of only 2.4 during the same period. Seventy-four percent of the anticipated growth in global urban population between 1950 and 2000 is expected to occur in the Third World with a breakdown of 13 percent in Africa, 16 percent in Latin America, 18 percent in East Asia, and 28 percent in South Asia.[3]·

The average annual growth rates of total, rural, and urban population are depicted in Table 1.2. The urban growth rates of the Third World countries have been, and are projected to continue to be, twice as high as the urban growth rate of the more developed nations and three times as high by the last decade of the century. By the end of the century the world urban population is projected to be in the neighborhood of 3.3 billion, an increase of approximately 145 percent.[4] During the period 1950-2000 world population is projected to grow by 160 percent and the urban population by 375 percent.[5]

In the 1950s Latin America and East Asia were the regions that experienced the most rapid urban growth. However, they have now been replaced by Africa. During the period 1975-80, urban areas in Africa were estimated to have grown at an annual rate of 5.1 percent. South Asia also experienced rising urban growth rates during the 1950-80 period, increasing steadily from an annual average of 3.37 percent during 1950-60 to 4.33 percent during 1975-80.[6]

Components of Urbanization

The significant growth of the urban population in the Third World today is the direct result of two major factors: natural increase of the urban population and rural-urban migration. Let us examine each component in detail, begining with the natural population increase.

TABLE 1.2

Average Annual Growth Rates of Total, Urban, and Rural Population
By Region, 1960-2000
(Percentages)

COMPONENT	1960	1965	1970	1975	1980	1985	1990	1995	2000
TOTAL POPULATION									
World Total	1.89	1.96	1.92	1.93	1.97	1.98	1.91	1.86	1.76
More Developed Regions	1.28	1.22	0.88	0.88	0.87	0.85	0.76	0.67	0.62
Less Developed Regions	2.18	2.31	2.39	2.36	2.39	2.37	2.29	2.22	2.08
URBAN POPULATION									
World Total	3.47	3.02	2.93	3.05	3.05	3.02	2.91	2.81	2.69
More Developed Regions	2.40	2.18	1.96	1.76	1.69	1.61	1.45	1.29	1.18
Less Developed Regions	5.01	4.09	4.07	4.38	4.29	4.15	3.95	3.76	3.53
RURAL POPULATION									
World Total	1.14	1.42	1.36	1.25	1.25	1.22	1.12	1.02	0.88
More Developed Regions	-0.18	-0.20	-0.93	-0.84	-0.94	-1.05	-1.21	-1.36	-1.47
Less Developed Regions	1.50	1.81	1.86	1.65	1.62	1.55	1.42	1.30	1.11

SOURCE: United Nations, Population Division, *Urban-Rural Projections From 1950 to 2000* (New York: United Nations, Working Paper No. 10, October 9, 1974).

Natural Population Increase

Despite the much larger pool of potential rural-urban migrants in the Third World, the rate of urban in-migration, on the whole, differs very little from that of the more developed countries. It is therefore fair to conclude that the causes of rapid urban growth in the Third World are closely linked to the causes of rapid natural increase, particularly in Latin American and South Asian countries.

In Table 1.3 we see that in half of the countries natural population increase was responsible for more than 50 percent of urban growth. Conversely, in the other half of the countries the natural population increase accounted for less than 50 percent of the urban growth. Demographers have shown that the proximate cause for today's rapid urban population growth in those countries with large natural increases of the urban population has been the postwar decline in mortality rates which increased the gap between fertility and mortality.

TABLE 1.3

Share of Urban Growth Due to Natural Population Increase
In Selected Third World Nations, 1970-75
(Percent)

COUNTRY	SHARE OF GROWTH DUE TO NATURAL INCREASE
PAPUA NEW GUINEA	26
TANZANIA	36
NIGERIA	36
COLOMBIA	57
MEXICO	77
THAILAND	55
SRI LANKA	39
INDIA	55

SOURCE: Kathleen Newland, *City Limits: Emerging Constraints on Urban Growth* (Washington, D.C.: Worldwatch Institute, 1980), p.10.

The primary factors in the decline in mortality in the world have been well documented and are better understood than the factors in the decline of fertility. The decrease in mortality was in large part the unanticipated and unplanned by-product of social, technological, economic, and political change.[7] The decrease in mortality was disproportionately achieved by lower infant and child mortality. Whereas, expectation of life at birth has greatly increased, doubling and more than doubling, that at age 60 has gone up relatively little. The reduced death rates in the Third World were also partly achieved exogenously as the result of technology and technical know-how imported from abroad. Thus, although it took the United States the first half of this century to cut its death rate in half, it took Sri Lanka, for example, less than a decade to do the same after World War II.[8]

Yet, despite the continued rapid decline in mortality in the Third World, there is alarming evidence that some causes of death believed to have been subjected to control have reappeared. For example, deaths attributed to malaria have increased as this disease has again become a health problem in a number of Third World nations in Asia and Africa.[9]

Mortality is the result of the interaction of three sets of factors affecting an individual's physical well-being. These are (1) public health services, such as immunization, which affect mortality regardless of individual behaviour; (2) health and environmental services (for example, clean water), which reduce the costs of health to individuals but require some individual response; and (3) an array of individual characteristics, including both income, which affects health through food consumption and housing, and education, which affects the speed and efficiency with which individuals respond to health and environmental services.[10] It is now argued that of these three sets of factors affecting mortality, the benefits of the first have been more or less fully harvested.[11] Further mortality declines depend therefore on changes in individual behaviour that are facilitated by increasing income and education and better access to health services.

However, mortality continued to decline in the Third World during the last decade, though not as quickly as it did during the previous twenty years. The Third World has now reached mortality rates of about 10 to 20 per 1,000 — rates which the developed countries did not attain until about 1900, and in some instances, even 1925.[12]

With the possible exception of Africa, the Third World has entered a phase of demographic transition. After significant reductions in mortality following World War II, many Third World countries are now experiencing a decline in fertility that may eventually lead to a new state of stationary population.[13] However, since the developed world reached replacement fertility in 1975 and its population is expected to grow very little then almost all future population growth will be contributed by the Third World. The size of the future population depends therefore upon future fertility changes in the Third World.

Fertility declines in the Third World began in the 1950s in a small group of countries that included Barbados, Guadeloupe, Mauritius, Puerto Rico, Singapore, Sri Lanka, and Trinidad and Tobago. In the early 1960s these areas were joined by another set of countries that included Chile, Costa Rica, Guyana, Malaysia, and South Korea. During the period 1965-75 fertility began to decline repidly in a wide range of Third World countries including Colombia, El Salvador, Indonesia, Jamaica, Mexico, Panama Thailand, Tunisia, and Venezuela.[14] More recently, and as seen in Table 1.4, there were further declines in several countries.

The timing of child bearing, as measured by current fertility rates for women in specific age groups, shows considerable variation in the Third World nations. In those countries where women marry young, fertility rates are high for women aged 15-19. Among women aged 40-44 and 45-49, low fertility rates exist in several Asian countries, including those with high overall fertility, such as Pakistan. Part of the explanation for this may be that in much of Asia there is a stigma attached to women who continue to have children after their own children have started childbearing; these older women have traditionally controlled their fertility through abstinence.[15] A few nations that portray substantial fertility declines, but still have a low age at marriage, tend to have peak fertility at ages 20-24; such countries include the Dominican Republic, Guyana, Jamaica, and Panama. In contrast, some high fertility countries, such as Jordan, Lesotho, and Syria have high fertility rates over a wider range, generally 20-34.[16]

TABLE 1.4

Total Fertility Rate in Selected Third World Nations
For 1975 and 1980

COUNTRY	TOTAL FERTILITY RATE	
	1975	1980
BANGLADESH	6.6	6.0
BURMA	5.5	5.3
INDIA	5.7	4.9
SRI LANKA	4.2	3.6
EL SALVADOR	6.2	5.7
PERU	5.8	5.0
JAMAICA	5.4	3.9
HONG KONG	3.0	2.2
VENEZUELA	5.3	4.5
SINGAPORE	2.8	1.8
BRAZIL	5.2	4.1
PHILIPPINES	6.4	4.6
COLOMBIA	5.9	3.8
TRINIDAD AND TOBAGO	3.4	2.6

SOURCES: World Bank, *World Development Reports 1978 and 1982*
(Washington D.C.: World Bank; and New York: Oxford University Press,
Respectively).

Fertility rates tend to be higher in rural than in urban populations in the Third World. The differential is more pronounced
and universal in Latin America. In Africa, Asia and the Pacific,
the differences are smaller and less widespread. When education
is taken into consideration, the fertility differentials are much
wider. As can be seen in Table 1.5, in general, the average number
of children per woman declines as the woman's level of education
increases. Female education bears one of the strongest negative
relationships to fertility. In the poorest countries, women with
some primary schooling have slightly higher fertility than women
with no education at all. Women with completed primary schooling, however, virtually always have lower fertility than those with
no schooling at all, and fertility declines monotonically as a
mother's education increases above primary schooling.[17] Higher
levels of educational attainment in the Third World also tend to

TABLE 1.5
Fertility Differentials by Education and Residence*

REGION AND COUNTRY	EDUCATION			RESIDENCE	
	NONE	PRIMARY	SECONDARY AND HIGHER	RURAL	URBAN
AFRICA					
Kenya	5.6	5.7	5.0	5.7	5.1
Lesotho	4.2[a]	4.0	2.9[a]	4.0	3.9
Senegal	5.4	5.1	3.1	5.3	5.2
Sudan (North)	4.9	5.8	3.9[a]	5.0	5.0
ASIA AND PACIFIC					
Bangladesh	5.7	5.7	4.9	5.7	5.6
Fiji	4.8	4.2	3.1	4.4	3.8
Indonesia	3.9	4.3	3.6	4.0	3.9
Malaysia	4.7	4.4	2.6	4.6	3.7
Nepal	4.1	3.5	3.5	4.1	4.0
Pakistan	5.0	5.2	3.9	4.8	5.4
Philippines	4.5	4.7	3.5	4.6	3.6
Sri Lanka	4.7	4.3	3.0	3.8	3.7
Thailand	4.8	3.9	2.2	4.1	3.0
LATIN AMERICA AND CARIBBEAN					
Colombia	5.9	4.6	3.1	5.5	4.0
Costa Rica	5.1	4.3	2.6	4.9	3.1
Dominican Republic	5.4	5.0	2.5	5.5	4.3
Guyana	5.5	5.1	3.6	5.3	4.1
Haiti	3.6	3.4	2.5	3.6	3.3
Jamaica	−b	4.5	2.2	4.8	3.5
Mexico	6.0	5.1	2.9	5.5	4.6
Peru	5.4	4.9	3.1	5.1	4.2
Trinidad and Tobago	−b	3.8	2.2	3.9	2.9
MIDDLE EAST					
Jordan	6.4	5.3	3.4	6.3	5.7
Syria	5.6	5.2	4.1	5.6	4.9

SOURCE: R. Lightbourne, S. Singh and C.P. Green, "The World Fertility Survey: Charting Global Childbearing," *Population Bulletin* 37 (March 1982), p. 22.

*Average number of children ever born per ever-married woman age 30-34.

[a]20-25 cases.

[b]Less than 20 cases.

reflect higher levels of economic well-being, which in turn influence and result in lower rates of fertility. Urban incomes are generally higher than rural incomes, often by a factor of three or more and a number of studies have shown that the wife's educational level is a better predictor of fertility than the husband's. In general, married women who work outside the home have smaller families than women who do not. According to data from the World Fertility Survey, women who work for nonfamilial employers have the lowest fertility, followed by women employed by their family and those who are self-employed; unemployed women have the highest fertility. Nonfamilial employment has a stronger effect on recent marital fertility in Latin America than it has in Asia and the Pacific.[18]

The key demographic factors that make for future natural urban population increase in the Third World are three-fold. First is the expected and continuing drop in mortality levels, which will in turn result in a substantial increase in life expectancy. These will largely offset fertility declines. The second factor is the very high proportion of children and youth in the general population, particularly in Latin America where 40 percent or more of the population is 15 years of age and younger. In the industrialized nations, between 22 and 25 percent of the population is 15 years old or younger. Thus, when those in this age group in Latin America enter their reproductive period of life, their sheer numbers will represent an awesome potential for further large population increases, regardless of the fact that the rate of increase may be diminishing. The third and final factor is time itself. A lengthy period is needed for a population structure to mature and attain a balance, which occurs when the death rate has passed through its transition period (from high to low levels), and the birth rate has done likewise. In time, the age structure will also evolve so that a larger proportion of the population is adult. Latin America, for example, finds itself near the midpoint in this process.[19] However, decades must elapse before the transition is completed in the Third World.

Rural-Urban Migration

Migration is the other important determinant of urban population growth. The usual focus is on the net migration from rural to urban areas, but also of importance are the urban-to-urban migra-

tion flows that take place in the Third World. The latter phenomenon is particularly important from the perspective of the smaller towns and intermediate-size cities that may be facing a net
migration outflow.[20]

In Tables 1.6 and 1.7 we see the share of net migration in
urban growth by region and selected countries, respectively.

TABLE 1.6

Average Annual Rate of Rural-Urban Transfers and Rural-Urban Transfers
As a Percentage of Urban Growth for Major Regions and Sub-Regions,
1950-60, 1970-75, and 1980-90

REGION	RURAL-URBAN TRANSFERS PER 1000 URBAN POPULATION			RURAL-URBAN TRANSFERS AS A PERCENTAGE OF URBAN GROWTH		
	1950-60	1970-75	1980-90	1950-60	1970-75	1980-90
WORLD TOTAL	16.7	9.3	9.3	48.7	32.5	33.0
DEVELOPED COUNTRIES	12.1	9.3	7.3	48.8	46.2	49.7
DEVELOPING COUNTRIES	29.2	17.1	16.4	59.3	42.0	42.2
AFRICA	28.6	21.9	18.1	56.3	45.2	38.7
East Africa	34.7	29.3	24.7	61.5	51.7	45.5
Middle Africa	70.3	35.7	25.3	78.7	61.1	48.8
North Africa	21.3	17.2	13.9	45.5	58.0	32.9
South Africa	13.4	10.6	10.9	36.2	28.3	28.0
West Africa	28.9	24.5	22.0	57.8	48.7	43.1
LATIN AMERICA	17.1	11.6	8.6	38.4	29.5	24.1
Caribbean	5.7	9.4	8.9	19.5	28.4	28.0
Tropical America	23.1	14.4	10.0	44.2	33.1	26.5
EAST ASIA	39.6	14.4	13.7	71.7	46.6	52.1
China	51.9	16.0	17.1	76.5	49.1	57.2
Japan	21.3	10.6	6.3	63.3	45.7	46.7
Other East Asia	25.5	21.1	13.9	47.9	49.5	41.2
SOUTH ASIA	15.6	17.1	17.3	43.1	40.0	41.0
South East Asia	24.0	19.5	18.7	52.0	42.0	42.3
Middle Asia	9.7	14.8	16.6	32.6	37.5	40.2
West Asia	28.7	19.1	12.6	52.7	40.0	69.5
OCEANIA	8.7	8.1	6.0	35.7	34.3	27.8
Melanesia	81.3	64.1	41.3	82.0	72.7	61.0
Micronesia	21.2	17.4	13.6	46.9	40.6	35.4

SOURCE: Sally Findley, *Planning for Internal Migration: A Review of Issues
and Policies in Developing Countries* (Washington, D.C.: U.S. Government
Printing Office, ISP-RD-4, 1977), p. 36.

In sub-Saharan Africa, where most of the cities are relatively small but growing very rapidly, migration from rural areas is the primary influence on urban growth. However, even in those nations where natural increase is the major source of urban growth, rural-urban migration makes a heavy contribution as well. Urban migrants contribute from one-third to one-half of the annual growth rate of Third World cities. Because the vast majority of migrants are young adults in the peak productive age groups with higher fertility than the urban population as a whole, the long-term contribution of internal migration to urban population growth is actually much greater.[21]

Table 1.7

Percentage Share of Net Migration in Urban Growth
In Selected Nations, 1970-75

COUNTRY	SHARE OF NET MIGRATION
ANGOLA	98.4
PAPUA NEW GUINEA	74.3
RWANDA	70.1
LESOTHO	67.2
NIGERIA	64.3
TANZANIA	64.0
SRI LANKA	60.5
HAITI	55.6
JAMAICA	52.6
INDIA	44.8
COLOMBIA	42.9
TRINIDAD AND TOBAGO	42.1
CUBA	37.9
COSTA RICA	34.2
GUATEMALA	20.0
MEXICO	23.9

SOURCES: Same as for Table 1.3; and Bertrand Renaud, *National Urbanization Policy in Developing Countries* (New York: Oxford University Press, 1981), pp. 165-166.

There are basically two models of the migration process. In the first, migration is regarded as a purposeful and rational search for a better place to live and work. In the second, migration is viewed as a response to conditions which push the migrant into moving, perhaps without a rational weighing of alternatives. The theoretical literature on migration determinants is well publicized and need not be reviewed in detail here.[22] However, it is important to discuss what the evidence from that literature suggests.

The various theories have stimulated considerable empirical activity and the results seem to be consistent. Although people migrate for a variety of reasons, the empirical evidence suggests very clearly that the primary factor determining migration is economic betterment. People migrate from rural to urban areas in response to perceived differences in economic opportunities between their original location and their final destination. Migrants tend to move from low to high income regions, and survey after survey finds that economic factors are most frequently cited as reasons for moving. These economic motives fall into two classes, the search for employment and the search for higher incomes. Additionally, the expectation of better education facilities for children is usually cited as a major reason for migration to the urban areas.

In addition to the predominant economic factors there are also some demographic factors that tend to influence migrant selectivity. Migrants are relatively young and tend to be between the ages of 15 and 30. In Latin America, migration is predominantly female while in Africa and South Asia it appears to be predominantly male.[23] Female migration to cities in Latin America is encouraged by the multitude of jobs available for women in domestic and other service activities. This age and sex selectivity reflects the lifecycle factors influencing migration. At certain stages in an individual's life there is a high likelihood of changing households and communities at the same time. Examples of such points in the lifecycle are when youth first leave the parental home in search of employment; upon marriage or divorce; and upon retirement.[24]

Another factor in migration selectivity is that of education. Migrants tend to be well educated and highly motivated relative to the population at the point of origin. Individuals with formal education, especially at the secondary level or higher, can obtain good jobs in government or commerce. These jobs are located in major urban centers and hence aspiring employees must migrate to these cities. Cities that receive migrants thus are not, on balance, burdened with a flood of uneducated, unskilled, and unmotivated individuals and households, although there is little doubt that rural-urban migration tends to keep urban wages below levels that would prevail in the absence of migration.[25]

Rural-urban migration continues to be the dominant net migration flow in nearly all Third World nations. Rapid rural-urban migration in the Third World presents both obstacles and opportunities to Third World cities. About 3 billion people live in the poor countries of Africa, Asia, and Latin America. Two-thirds of this total live almost entirely in non-Communist Third World nations, and of these, 40 to 50 percent or about 800 million to 1 billion people, are the truly poor. From one-fourth to one-half or even more of these people live in the slums, shanty towns, and streets of the Third World's cities - Lima, Georgetown, Bombay, Bogota - giving rise to what is now regarded as the "urban dilemma".

Consequences of Urbanization

Until a few years ago economists, sociologists, and social planners alike regarded urbanization as being positively associated with higher productivity and industrialization. Proponents of the thesis that large cities have a positive role in development had pointed to, the advantages that firms or business receive from access to larger markets for their products as well as for labour and other inputs; the advantages that urban residents enjoy in terms of access to better social services; and the value of the more organized participation in the political process that comes with increased urbanization.[26]

However, in contrast to this viewpoint, it is now persuasively clear that there are negative effects and some costs associated with the concentration of economic activity and population in the urban areas of the Third World. The "overurbanization" that results is associated with widespread unemployment and underemployment in addition to all of the problems of lack of housing and access to urban services, traffic congestion, and environmental pollution.

The principal measurements of how well urban areas in Third World countries have absorbed the rapid population growth are estimates of urban unemployment and underemployment. One of the major consequences of the rapid urbanization experienced by Third World nations in the past two decades has been the increasing supply of urban job seekers. In many countries the supply of job seekers far exceeds demand, and this situation results in extremely high rates of unemployment, as seen in Table 1.8, and underemployment in the urban areas. When account is taken of the underemployment rate, which exceeds 25 percent in Latin America, Asia and Africa, then the overall figure for urban surplus labour well exceeds 30 percent in many Third World nations.[27]

Recent research further points out that open unemployment in urban areas is a more serious problem for those 15 to 24 years old than for the total labour force, for females than for males, and, at least up to a postsecondary level of education, for the more educated than for the less educated.[28]

Some studies have shown that the migrant portion of the urban population have lower rates of unemployment than the natives, possibly because they accept jobs which natives will not take. Low unemployment rates among migrants may or may not lead to increased unemployment among natives. If the jobs are really ones that natives do not take, natives unemployment levels may be unaffected.[29] This is an important issue, however, since it brings into question the popular assumption that migrants raise urban unemployment levels through either their own unemployment or their taking jobs away from natives.

Despite the fact that average household incomes tend to be systematically higher in urban than in rural areas and tend to be positively associated with city size, in the cities, underemployment and unemployment have a negative income impact on the family and often contribute to its instability. Since the mother and other family members leave home to work, this creates a situation in which children and young people lose some adult supervision. Often the children themselves must find work; and if they do, they also leave home at an early age, which in turn makes for the

Table 1.8

Urban and Rural Unemployment Rates in Selected Countries

COUNTRY	YEAR	UNEMPLOYMENT RATE(%)		RATIO OF URBAN TO RURAL UNEMPLOYMENT RATES
		URBAN	RURAL	
KOREA	1965	12.7	3.1	4.1
PANAMA	1967	9.3	2.8	3.3
CHILE	1968	6.1	2.0	3.1
INDONESIA	1971	4.8	1.8	2.7
TAIWAN	1968	3.5	1.4	2.5
VENEZUELA	1968	6.5	3.1	2.1
PHILIPPINES	1967	13.1	6.9	1.9
TRINIDAD AND TOBAGO	1971	16.5	8.7	1.9
TANZANIA	1965	7.0	3.9	1.8
INDIA	1972-73	6.7	3.9	1.7
MALAYSIA	1967	11.6	7.4	1.6
SYRIA	1967	7.3	4.6	1.6
SRI LANKA	1968	14.8	10.4	1.4

SOURCE: Johannes F. Linn, *Cities in the Developing World: Policies For Their Equitable and Efficient Growth* (New York: Oxford University Press, 1983), p. 7.

disintegration of the family unit. One effect of urbanization has too often been the abandonment of children as traditional value systems erode. Employment and poverty in urban settings clearly have different effects on family structures from those found in rural areas.[30]

The rapid process of urbanization in the Third World has given rise to concern regarding the costs of urbanization. The uncontrolled and unplanned urban growth makes it difficult for cities to provide residents with the services they desire despite the current urban bias with respect to development expenditures and strategies. Urbanization is decisive because it is expensive. The difference between the costs of urban development and rural development turns on infrastructure. Urban housing, for example, is much more expensive than rural housing. The proportion of urban children for whom schooling is provided is always much higher than in rural areas. Moreover, rural residents do more for themselves with their own resources than do urban residents.[31]

There are four common, but distinct, reasons for concern over the costs of urbanization in the Third World. These are as follows:

(1) "Fiscal - Urbanization places a heavy burden on governments as they have to meet the rapidly rising demands for urban services.

(2) Financial - The high financial costs of urbanization are believed to be the prime cause of the heavy and growing international indebtedness of Third World nations.

(3) Efficiency - The economic costs of urbanization (including congestion and pullution costs) are taken to exceed those of rural growth; this in turn is taken as a basis for judging urban development excessive in terms of economic efficiency.

(4) Equity - Rural households are thought to subsidize high urbanization costs."[32]

The conclusions on these four considerations as determined by Linn[33] are: It is impossible to derive an overall judgement about how aggregate public service costs vary with settlement size. Despite the fact that urbanization imposes a rapidly growing fiscal burden on Third World governments, there is little reason to suspect that reducing the urbanization process *per se* will reduce this burden unless it is accompanied by reduced rates of industrialization or reduced population and income growth. With respect to financial considerations, it was found that rapid urbanization was not the primary cause of international indebtedness of the Third World nations. There is simply no statistical correlation between urbanization rates and debt ratios. In terms of efficiency considerations, costs alone were found not to influence the optimum degree of urbanization or optimum size of cities. Benefits have to be taken into consideration also. Moreover, many of the apparent symptoms of urban inefficiency, in particular congestion and pollution, are due to inappropriate policies within the city rather than the result of inefficient city size or inefficiently high rates of urbanization. Finally, with respect to equity considerations, it was found that rural dwellers do not necessarily subsidize urbanization costs. Where this may be the case the cause was found to be inequitable public pricing and tax policies.

The above conclusions not withstanding, however, other evidence suggests that the rapid growth of urban areas has far outpaced the ability of Third World governments to provide adequate services.[34] There is evidence that air pollution, noise levels, congestion, crime, and health problems tend to increase more than proportionately with the size of urban centers.[35] Urban living has increased both the quantity and the quality of the economic needs and desires of the population. Such changes are very important since they raise individual expectations and impose added constraints on the economic policies of governments.

Pollution, congestion, lack of adequate services, and urban sprawl are experienced by urban centers in both developed and Third World nations. However, there is a fundamental difference based on degree. Urbanization in the Third World has occurred at a much more rapid pace and most of their cities have been unable to meet the growing demand for housing and urban services. Such urban growth is expected to continue into the foreseeable future even if national policy biases favouring urbanization are corrected. Consequently, the degree of efficiency with which Third World nations allocate their resources will increasingly determine their overall economic performance.

Policies to Manage Rapid Urbanization

Third world governments have not succeeded in planning urban growth, which has taken place more or less quite spontaneously. The solution to this urbanization problem requires the adaptation of current Third World urban growth to the limitations imposed by each country's available resources. This type of adaptation ought to result in an "appropriate" city. Such appropriateness implies that the development of urban strategy should be designed so as to cover the maximum number of the existing population.

Despite the fact that it may be very late to bring about important changes in the larger cities, the inevitable urban growth that will be affecting cities of all sizes in the next two or three decades means that there will be repeated opportunities for doing better before patterns are so set as to become irreversible. As such, appropriate national urbanization policies must be given priority in the Third World and must include four major objectives: the full development of the national resources of the country; the maintenance of national cohesion among various regions, particularly in the case of very large disparities in per capita output among regions; the prevention or correction of excessive concentration of economic activities within the urban regions; and the more efficient and more equitable growth management within cities.[36]

National urbanization policies will be influenced from country to country by the economic, social, political, and cultural characteristics that exist within each country. Countries differ widely with respect to their national urban systems and these differences imply dissimilar urbanization policies. For example, the strategy to combat a high primacy pattern such as in Thailand would be inappropriate for a country with a more balanced spatial structure such as Nigeria or Malaysia. Also, policies would vary between high urbanization regions such as Latin America and low urbanization regions such as Africa and most of Asia. In general, the lower the current level of urbanization the greater the scope for a national urbanization policy in the sense of flexibility in changing the urban size distribution.[37]

It follows then that national urbanization policies must include elements that reduce urban unemployment and narrow the rural-urban wage gap; increase the relative disposition of the public services in the urban centers; foster integrated rural development; and improve administrative responsiveness.

Urban Job Creation and the Elimination of Urban Biases

The primary cause of urban poverty in the Third World is the severely limited income earned by the poor through gainful employment. Policies designed to increase the employment and wages of the urban poor must therefore be given foremost attention. The basic issue to be dealt with therefore is how the urban labour supply can be absorbed at decent wages without further increasing the urban-rural wage differential.

Perhaps the most powerful stimulus to job creation, and hence labour demand, is economic growth. Economic growth leads to rapid labour absorption throughout the economy in both urban and rural areas alike. Conversely, when an economy stagnates, as is currently the case in both the Third World and developed nations, unemployment is a much more pressing problem. Policies aimed at improving the economic growth of a nation are therefore very important elements of any employment strategy. However, such macroeconomic policies by themselves cannot eliminate the general employment problem in the Third World. Clearly, there will need to be supplementary policies that bring about the growth of the manufacturing, service, and government activities sectors. Policies designed to generate a rapid and sustainable growth in these sectors will therefore also lead to a rapid growth in the demand for urban labour.

With respect to urban-wage biases, wage rates have consistently been higher in the urban areas. Wage rates in rural areas are usually thought to be determined either by subsistence or nutritional requirements or else by the forces of supply and demand, the latter explanation entailing competition, dualism and monopsony. Efforts to narrow the rural-urban wage gap usually involve incomes policies to keep urban wage rates from rising and price supports for agricultural products to raise incomes, as in Kenya. Some nations, such as Singapore, have also exercised wage restraint by curtailing the power of the trade unions. Since 1953 India has sought to moderate wage demands through labour courts, wage boards, and industrial tribunals. Other countries, such as Tanzania, have used public sector wage scales. But perhaps what is needed is a freeze on urban real wage rates, particularly in the public sector, either through a modification of civil service salary scales or by allowing urban prices and taxes to accelerate disproportionately to rural prices and taxes.[38] Unless such concrete efforts are made to moderate the rural-urban wage differential then migration from the rural to the urban areas will continue to be a rational decision for achieving economic betterment.

Improving Urban Public Services

Rapid urbanization in the Third World has made it difficult for governments to provide, in a timely and efficient manner, all of the public services urban residents need. The combination of urban congestion and inadequate services generates health, education, transportation, and housing problems.

Education and Health Policy: Government involvement in the provision of social services such as education and health has been a long-standing practice in the Third World. On average, urban households are more educated, healthier, and better served by education and health facilities than their rural counterparts. The urban poor, however, usually have limited access to the better health care centers and schools in the urban areas due to the prohibitive costs. To combat this situation a number of countries, notably in the Caribbean, have implemented systems of universal education and health care to ensure access for everyone, regardless of income level or social stratum. These countries must be commended and such a universalized system of education and health care ought to be attempted in other Third World nations as an effort towards meeting basic human needs in those nations.

Every individual is born with a collection of abilities and talents. Education, in its many forms, has the potential to help fulfill and apply them while the widespread provision of basic preventive and curative medical services is essential to the life expectancy of all individuals.

Recognition of the link between education and development has led to public expenditures on education becoming very important in many nations when measured in relation to Gross National Product. For a number of Third World nations, education absorbed more than a quarter of all public expenditures. More and more education is being placed in the overall context of development objectives as one of the many important policy instruments to alleviate the rapid urbanization problem.

Three separate but interrelated perspectives illustrate the significance of education to development.[39] First, it is a basic human need. It provides people with fundamental knowledge, skills, values, and attitudes while enhancing their capacity to change and their willingness to accept new ideas. In the Third World, education is becoming increasingly necessary for survival. It assists people in understanding and benefiting from change and to persevere in attaining their economic rights. Second, education is seen as a means of meeting other basic needs mainly because it provides the necessary knowledge for change in current practices and skills to better use the services provided. Increased productivity and greater longevity arising directly out of education raise the demand for better housing, more food, cleaner water, and more educational and health facilities while also enabling society as a whole to better satisfy such needs. The relationship is reciprocal. Thirdly, education also plays a critical role for development by providing individuals with the ability to change their culture and to seek constructive roles in society.

Improving health in the Third World requires efforts far beyond medical care. It is closely linked with food and nutrition, with employment and income distribution, and with the international economy. In general terms, the determinants of health have long been well known. One is people's purchasing power over certain goods and services, including food, housing, fuel, soap, water, and medical services. Another is the health environment - climate, standards of public sanitation and the prevalence of communicable diseases. A third is people's understanding of nutrition, health and hygiene.[40]

The 1970s have witnessed the evolution of a much broader approach to health policy, including attempts to implement universal low-cost basic health care. However, primary and preventive health care is still not a nationwide reality in most Third World nations. In fact, public health expenditures in the Third World are heavily biased in favour of curative care, and within this category the emphasis is on in-hospital rather than out-patient care despite the prevalence of diseases whose incidence could be greatly reduced by preventive measures. The proportion of public health expenditures on preventive health care is rarely above 20 percent although there is considerable variation among countries.[41] The diversion of public resources to hospitals that provide high quality care for relatively few people rather than environmental sanitation and mass immunization is a costly social waste at the expense of the poor. There is a long list of diseases to which the poor are particularly susceptible and which can be prevented by the better provision of environmental sanitation projects, piped water, and insecticides.[42]

Health policy in the Third World should therefore reverse existing priorities and, indeed, there is some indication that this is beginning to take place. In Indonesia and the Philippines, for example, recent health care projects have emphasized comprehensive preventive care. But perhaps the framework of the basic health care system in Jamaica provides the best example for Third World nations of a comprehensive primary health care system. The system operates out of community-based health centers in locations easily accessible to the poor; it relies primarily on out-patient treatment; it emphasizes preventive health care and education (slanted toward the needs of such vulnerable groups as pregnant mothers, infants, and children), improved sanitation, maternal and infant care, immunization, family planning, and nutrition programs; and it is supported by a relatively inexpensive but effective paramedical staff.[43]

Transportation Policy: Transportation is typically a means to other ends, in both its passenger and freight aspects. It plays a central role in the development of urban areas as the essential link between residence and employment, and between producers and users of goods and services. Traffic congestion inevitably occurs as urban areas grow due to the fact that transport facilities cannot be expanded enough to maintain mobility, partly because of resource limitations and also partly because urban transport demand is not curtailed by pricing or regulation. The private automobile takes roughly nine times more road space per passenger than does a bus. The explosive increase in automobiles in the urban areas of the Third World, at rates two to five times those of urban populations, therefore exerts tremendous demands on the existing urban road space, and is a major cause of severe congestion and pollution problems, especially in the cities of the middle-income countries,[44] such as Port-of-Spain in Trinidad and Tobago.

The poor are mostly affected by the transportation dilemma in the Third World both in terms of the cost and their dependence on it for access to employment and services. As such, usually any disruptions in transportation service will create severe hardships for this already hard pressed group.

Past transportation policies in the Third World have been, and continue to be in some countries, oriented towards private automobile traffic primarily in the urban centers. This resulted in massive expenditures on urban roads and to the neglect of strategies to develop bus and train facilities and access roads for low-income neighborhoods. Considerable scope therefore exists for revising current transportation policies and replacing them with policies that would, *inter alia,* control private automobile operation and ownership; emphasize mass transit facilities; help conserve energy and foreign exchange; increase employment; improve access for the poor; impose user fee charges for cost recovery of public transportation investments; encourage private service provision and/or de-nationalize mass transit facilities; and enforcement of national regulations that maintain order and accountability.

Housing Policy: The need for housing is fundamental. But many Third World nations have not been able to give it priority. It has been estimated that more than half of the population in principal cities in forty Third World countries live in slums and uncontrolled settlements in seventeen of the cities; only twelve of the cities has less than a third of the population living in these conditions.[45] The high concentration and visibility of deficiencies in urban housing make this one of the most urgent problems facing Third World nations in their transition from rural to urban societies with the ultimate result being a shortage of adequate housing which leads to overcrowding, squatter settlements, and steeply climbing housing prices.

Many Third World nations have developed public housing programs. Most of these efforts have failed because they were poorly located, built, or designed, and often too costly for the poor. Additionally, there can be no serious housing policy for the poor without a bold land policy, and such a land policy faces grave political obstacles. Often, construction of public housing has been combined with slum clearance programs. This is usually regarded as the solution to the slum's social by-product by doing away with them easily and quickly. Yet, in most cases slum clearance has been of little help, and even detrimental to efforts to provide housing.

Several countries have constructed residential estates located some distance from the urban centers. These housing estates serve to decongest the city and take advantage of lower land prices outside the city. Yet, housing estates suffer from many of the ills of public housing, namely poor transportation links; inappropriate design; and high rents.[46] Other countries have attempted to cope with housing shortages by promoting self-help or cooperative schemes as was the case in Guyana, for example, during the 1970s. This option is not without its problems, however. This type of construction is dependent on mutual cooperation and the participatory process which cannot be guaranteed for the duration of the construction. Moreover, there is also considerable dependence on the government for permits, licences, and foreign exchange releases to acquire materials, all of which are subject to bureaucratic discretion and tend to be under the control of corrupt officials who have to be bribed.

Housing policy in the Third World undoubtedly requires government intervention so that large numbers of the poor can benefit. The policy must contain elements that eliminate obstacles to private construction efforts; results in improvements in the availability of housing finance; encourages the upgrading of slums; and regulates the acquisition of land so that competition and equal opportunity is maintained.

Developing the Rural Sector

The bulk of the poor in the Third World live in the rural areas. Urban poverty is, however, more obvious - the slums and degradation of some cities in the Third World force themselves upon the notice of the richest citizen and upon the most casual visitor from other areas. But the bulk of the slum inhabitants and squatters on the streets have migrated to towns because they are pushed out of the rural areas by landlessness, joblessness, and hopelessness. It is therefore in the rural areas that the long-term problems of urban poverty can most effectively be tackled. Trying to confront mass poverty by only improving conditions and providing work in the urban centers simply attracts more people from the depressed rural areas.[47]

The development of the rural sector is therefore essential not only in terms of local improvement but also as a part of the overall national economic policy. Rural development is taken here to mean the far-reaching transformation of social and economic institutions, structures, relationships and processes in any rural area. It conceives the cardinal aim of rural development not simply as agricultural and economic growth in the narrow sense, but as balanced social and economic development - including the generation of new employment; the equitable distribution of income; widespread improvement in health, nutrition, and housing; greatly broadened opportunities for all individuals to realize their full potential through education and a strong voice for all the rural people in shaping the decisions and actions that affect their lives.[48]

For rural development to be successful it must be integrative in nature. Integrated rural development, as a concept, was first introduced by the donor agencies in the 1960s. It referred to particular types of projects designed to meet the requirements of simultaneous and comprehensive action in such areas as water, power, extension, credit, roads, and storage. The idea was that the various complementary activities of rural development required a single administrative framework rather than being implemented by a variety of separate agencies. The success of such projects in raising productivity and incomes in particular areas helped to popularize the slogan of integrated rural development which became the subject of a number of international conferences and seminars in the 1960s and 1970s.

The essential thrust of rural development is action to raise the level of living of the rural poor. Specific means for doing so encompass a wide range of approaches, which, if they are to be successful, must be adapted to the existing country situation; be realistic in terms of implementation; and supported by the policy makers. In attempting to achieve all of these goals, particular attention must be given to all aspects of the population situation since it is only through balances and coordinated efforts to increase production and services and to control population growth that significant improvements in living standards can be achieved in the Third World. Such integrated development is particularly important since much of the unemployed and underemployed rural labour force together with substantial new additions to the labour force must be retained in rural areas, if the problems of the urban areas are not to be exacerbated through uncontrolled migration to them.

Rural development strategies focus particularly, but not exclusively, on the agricultural sector due to the fact that agricultural activity is the major economic activity in the rural areas of the Third World. Debates over development strategy have often swirled around the relative importance to be assigned to agriculture versus industry. The historical evidence suggests that this dichotomy is frequently overstated. Specifically, the notion that rapid industrialization entails a total neglect of agriculture is erroneous; it underestimates the importance of the mutually beneficial links between agriculture and industrial development and indeed, in most Third World nations, successful industrialization has been supported by sustained and broadly-based agricultural growth. The major issues in agricultural development in Third World nations are how to sustain a rate of growth that allows for a balanced expansion of all parts of the economy, and how to ensure that the pattern of agricultural growth is such as to make a strong and direct impact on rural poverty and, indirectly, on the reduction of migration of the poor to urban areas. In the struggle towards industrialization it has been relatively easy to overlook the importance of the agricultural sector in development and to neglect the necessary harmony between policies to encourage the growth of industry and the performance of agriculture. But, despite the recent rapid rise of industry and the growing urbanization, the agricultural sector still looms large in the Third World since it is the sector which provides employment for a large section of the labour force; contains the majority of poor people; and is the birthplace of many of the urban poor.[49]

A rural development strategy may enter into the planning process at some or all of the following levels: the aggregate level, the sectoral level, the project level, and at the level of special measures loosely linked with the main structure of the plan. The majority of the Third World nations have acquired a great deal of experience in formulating development plans and, as such, the inclusion of a rural development strategy in these plans should pose no major problem. Realization of the objectives of a broad based integrated rural development strategy, however, hinges on national commitment and on the translation of that commitment into three areas of action. First, there must be the necessary policy changes, including more equitable distribution of land rights and incentive pricing for crops produced by subsistence farmers, in particular for food crops. Second, resources must be allocated on a priority basis to increase the productivity of the subsistence rural sector to develop agricultural technology, effective extension, and transportation networks. Third, an adequate effort must be geared to developing institutional capability, not only in the organized public sector but also in the rural agricultural sector to use to the maximum the existing resources and thus ensure effective implementation of the policies and plans directed at the unemployed.

Fundamental to any process of planned rural development is the active and willing participation of rural peoples in the development of the area in which they reside.[50] Such participation requires that these people not only share in the distribution of the benefits of development, be they the material benefits of increased output or other benefits considered enhancing to the quality of life, but that they share also in the task of creating these benefits. Participation may be regarded as a substitute for political mobilization. It is, in that sense, therefore, the antithesis of politicization. It provides, optimally, political legitimization for institutional programs without significant conflict.[51] This then serves to enhance the viability and success of the program or programs.

Land Reform: Land reform is one of the most relevant institutional factors in agricultural and rural development. Land reform can be regarded as a systematic, policy-directed change in the terms under which the agricultural population holds and uses land. The objectives are, generally, to improve the farming population's performance as well as its economic and social position. Essentially, land reform seeks to redistribute rights in land for the benefit of small farmers and agricultural labourers.[52] Since land reform, in the sense of redistribution of land, involves a conflict of interest between "haves" and "have-nots", it is also a political question. As a matter of fact, the immediate issues are more political than economic. Guyana's nationalization of the country's sugar estates is a prime example.

The benefits of any vigorous land reform program are many. First, the transfer of land from large properties into small ownership can be expected to lead to an increase in agricultural production, as a result of higher inputs of labour owing to its higher marginal productivity. An essential reason for the continued success of agricultural development after land reform is, as generally recognized, in the production incentive it gives small-scale own-account workers. Also, when production increases in the wake of land reform, more of it is likely to stay in the rural area as farmers' incomes. The whole incentive theory of land reform as a factor causing production to increase assumes that this happens, and so the agricultural population ought to become better off. At least in the short run, this should also mean better off in relation to the people in other sectors. This characteristic is one that leads to increased distributive equity in agriculture which may carry over into other sectors, and could conceivably be one of the more important, as yet overlooked, aspects of land reform.[53]

Given this normal level of expectation pertaining to incomes and production, then reform can be compatible with development, though the change in structure in itself is not likely to generate a higher rate of growth. In the Third World, it is necessary that attempts be made to derive some of these advantages. Essentially, land reform provides the landless rural classes and small owners with new opportunities to better their lot. Higher incomes will result in their being able to have more food, better housing and clothing, and a greater chance to educate themselves and remove themselves from the poverty rolls. The experience in countries that have undertaken land reform is encouraging in this respect. For example, in Mexico, China, Republic of Korea, and Japan such programs have substantially improved the rural income distribution, farmers' equity and security, and the base for subsequent agricultural progress.[54]

Public Investments: A program of public investment, and particularly of labour-intensive rural public works, is an essential component of a strategy to develop the rural sector. However, in countries where the distribution of the ownership of land is highly skewed, land reform makes it much easier to devise opportunities for productive investments in which benefits accrue mainly to the poor, that is in which the leakages are relatively small. Without land reform, leakages are likely to be large for most forms of public investment.

In any case, it is likely to be both desirable and feasible for governments to undertake labour-intensive rural public works programs for the two-fold purpose of providing supplementary income-earning opportunities for the most disadvantaged rural families and improving the rural infrastructure through the building of roads and similar activities.[55] Rural public investment is important precisely because it can be organized at the community level. Additionally, such investment revitalizes the rural lifestyle and creates a social and physical infrastructure which allows rural residents to share broadly in a nation's development benefits and remove them from the drudgery, isolation, and poor quality of life which has so often acted as a partial catalyst for migration to the urban centers. Examples of successful rural public works programs are the Inpres program of Indonesia and Morocco's Promotion Nationale program.

Participation of the Rural Poor: President Julius Nyerere of Tanzania has argued that..."If the people are to be able to develop they must have power. They must be able to control their own activities within the framework of their village communities. The people must participate not just in the physical labour involved in economic development but also in the planning of it and the determination of priorities."[56] Projects of genuine social and economic value are most likely to be identified, planned, and built if rural people are able to play a decisive role in choosing them. One author has argued that optimum participation must be included among development's strategic principles because unless efforts are made to widen participation, development will interfere with man's quest for esteem and freedom from manipulation.[57]

That higher levels of participation of the poor should and do generally have positive effects on socio-economic equality in the Third World is a foregone conclusion. More generally, widespread participation generally means more widespread access to power, and those who gain access to power will insist that there be actions to broaden their share in the economic benefits of society. In Jamaica, for example, participation of the poor in rural development is closely tied to the benefits that members derive therefrom.[58] And, in China, where the Socialist Revolution was based on a large-scale participation of the peasants in a revolutionary struggle, economic cooperation in agriculture and side-line production were combined with the lowest level of government administration and the principles of collective ownership of land and collective land use and considerably strengthened the autonomous power of these local units of rural administration.[59]

Additionally, there are large and growing numbers of peasant community organizations in such countries as Haiti, Paraguay, and Peru through which the rural poor are striving to improve their situations, and, their endurance in the face of great odds suggests the importance of the participatory process to them and their communities.[60]

But, despite the advocacy of the participatory process in the development literature and not withstanding its successful implementation in some countries, there still exists a number of obstacles to participation of the poor in the rural development process in the Third World. The obstacles faced are varied and are found within the implementing agencies, within the rural communities themselves, and also within the broader institutions of the society.[61] Within the implementing agencies, the primary problem is their centralized nature which does not lend itself to participation in decision-making by others. Moreover, these agencies tend to be located some distance away in national or regional capitals which keeps them out of touch with the rural communities they are intended to serve. In the rural communities themselves, the major problems are a lack of appropriate local organization and corruption on the part of the more powerful community individuals who take personal advantage of any latitude for influence available, thus corrupting the purpose of the participatory approach and destroying the spirit of cooperative effort. Within the broader society, the basic problem is that participation is generally pursued as a way of reaching the poorer elements of a society to increase their welfare. however, this involves a societal change process which tends to conflict with the *status quo.*[62]

It follows therefore that for the participatory process to be effective both political and economic power must be held by the people within their communities. The rural residents are in the best position to choose which organizations they will participate in. Experience shows that effective participation cannot be commanded by policy-makers but must instead be induced through the advocacy of projects that offer sufficient incentives to attract the personal resources of time; energy; and the freedom of action, away from other urgent and competing tasks, of the poor.

Improving Administrative Responsiveness

Institutional management in the Third World has historically been very poor despite the fact that institutional constraints are as serious a barrier to development as a shortage of development finance. The administrative machinery of Third World nations is generally located in the urban areas in isolation from the rural population and it tends to cater primarily to the needs of the urban residents.

Administrative and management capability in the Third World are hampered by a great many factors, primary among which is the transformation of the civil service into a bureaucratic organization where the sovereignty of politics rather then the supremacy of administration is emphasized.[63] Politics has become the most important activity and politicians have come to occupy a position of unquestionable supremacy in matters of decision-making. Bureaucratic power has shifted from the technical development administrator to the politician. At the same time, political interest has developed in personnel matters and this has deteriorated into nepotism, pork-barrel appointments, and the denial of jobs to non-supporters of the government. All of this has created a centralized and politicized bureaucracy resulting in a mass exodus of the most talented and qualified of the civil servants which has further resulted in a shortage of skilled personnel to manage development programs. Additionally, the civil service in Third World nations has a reputation for being tardy, lacking proper inter-departmental as well as intra-departmental communication, and deficient in its productivity.

Most Third World nations are well aware of the need to improve administrative performance, and some of them have undertaken some form of administrative and management reform programs. Administrative reform requires the direct relating of pertinent measures to national plan objectives, strategies, sectors, and programs in the plan itself. Described as "administrative and management planning", it calls for spelling out and providing for specific administrative and management requirements for implementing development plans concurrently with preparation of their economic, social and technical analyses and components. The common objectives of such reform planning include decentralizing the bureaucracy; promoting effective coordination and communication; instituting manpower planning and training; and changing the nature of the political leadership so that it becomes responsive to improving administrative and management performance.

Conclusions

Urban populations in many Third World nations are growing at rates far in excess of current labour absorption rates. Despite the fact that the natural increase of the urban population contributes the major portion of the urban growth, rural-urabn migration continues to be a significant factor. The primary factors influencing the decision to migrate are jobs and wages. However, economic betterment is not necessarily sufficient cause for migration. Social, educational, and some personal factors may also play a strong role in determining the incidence and timing of migration.

Unquestionably, an urban bias exists in the Third World. The urban sector in the Third World receives a disproportionately large share of government expenditures and capital investments. Also, the bulk of the Third World's social services are located in the cities, particularly in the large metropolitan areas although, for example, such things as urban transportation fares are subsidized by the entire population out of general revenues. This type of differential treatment, in turn, confirms and strengthens the reality of the city as the dynamic sector of the nation.

Underlying this trend are the unresolved rural development problems. A brief list of them would include a lack of sufficient progress on land reform policy; the low wages paid to rural workers; the repeated periods of unemployment and underemployment; the lack of agricultural credit for small landowners; and the isolation of rural communities without potable water, electricity, medical, educational or other services considered essential by urban residents.

Additionally, innovation, ingenuity and reform are also needed in urban administration and financing. The expanding urban sector requires increasingly sophisticated administration and financing systems if efficiency and innovation in the provision of services are to be obtained. Reliance on professional administration rather than political ones; the creation of careers in development management; the strengthening of urban tax bases; and the rationalization of expenditures are all formidable tasks for the Third World. Ideally, the accomplishment of these tasks ought to be attempted within the framework of a national urbanization policy as discussed earlier.

Notes

1. United Nations, *Patterns of Urban and Rural Population Growth* (New York: United Nations Population Studies No. 68, 1980), pp. 33-34.

2. Kathleen Newland, *City Limits: Emerging Constraints on Urban Growth* (Washington, D.C.: Worldwatch Paper 38, Worldwatch Institute, 1980), p.7.

3. United Nations, *Patterns of Urban and Rural Population Growth*, p.12.

4. Bertrand Renaud, *National Urbanization Policy in Developing Countries* (New York: Oxford University Press, 1981), p.15

5. *Ibid.*

6. United Nations, *Patterns of Urban and Rural Population Growth*, pp. 12-13.

7. United Nations, *The Determinants and Consequences of Population Trends* (New York: United Nations, 1973), Chapter V.

8. Philip M. Hauser, "Introduction and Overview" in P. Hauser (ed.) *World Population and Development* (Syracuse: Syracuse University Press, 1979), p. 15.

9. See Rafael M. Salas, "The State of the World Population, 1978", *Annual Report on UNFPA Activities and Plans to the Governing Council* (New York: United Nations, 1978).

10. Nancy Birdsall, *Population and Poverty in the Developing World* (Washington, D.C.: World Bank Staff Working Paper No. 404, 1980), p. 16.

11. See Jacques Loup, *Can the Third World Survive?* (Baltimore: Johns Hopkins University Press, 1983), pp. 61-65.

12. *Ibid.,* p.4.

13. *Ibid.,* p. 61.

14. William W. Murdoch, *The Poverty of Nations* (Baltimore: Johns Hopkins University Press, 1980), p. 87.

15. R. Lightbourne, S. Singh, and C.P. Green, "The World Fertility Survey: Charting Global Childbearing", *Population Bulletin* 37 (March 1982), p. 20.

16. *Ibid.*

17. See Susan H. Cochrane, *Fertility and Education: What Do We Really know?* (Baltimore: Johns Hopkins University Press, 1979).

18. R. Lightbourne, S. Singh, and C.P. Green, "The World Fertility Survey: Charting Global Childbearing", pp. 23-24.

19. Inter-American Development Bank, *Economic and Social Progress in Latin America 1979* (Washington, D.C.: IDB, 1979), p. 127.

20. Johannes F. Linn, *Cities in the Developing World: Policies for their Equitable and Efficient Growth* (New York: Oxford University Press, 1983), p. 44.

21. Michael P. Todaro, "Urbanization in Developing Nations: Trends, Prospects, and Policies", *Journal of Geography* 79 (September/October 1980), p. 169.

22. See for example, Michael P. Todaro, *Internal Migration in Developing Countries* (Geneva: ILO, 1976); Lorene Y.L. Yap, "The Attraction of Cities: A Review of the Migration Literature", *Journal of Development Economics* 4 (September 1977), pp. 239-264; and Sally Findley, *Planning for Internal Migration: A Review of Issues and Policies in Developing Countries* (Washington, D.C.: U.S. Government Printing Office, ISP-RD-4, 1977).

23. Bryan Roberts, *Cities of Peasants: The Political Economy of Urbanization in the Third World* (Beverly Hills: Sage Publications, 1978), p.100.

24. Sally Findley, *Planning for Internal Migration: A Review of Issues and Policies in Developing Countries,* pp. 13-14.

25. Johannes F. Linn, *Cities in the Developing World: Policies for Their Equitable and Efficient Growth,* p. 44.

26. Carmen A. Miro and Joseph E. Potter, *Population Policy: Research Priorities in the Developing World* (New York: St. Martin's Press, 1980), p.124.

27. Michael P. Todaro, "Urbanization in Developing Nations: Trends, Prospects, and Policies", p. 169.

28. Lyn Squire, *Employment in Developing Countries; A Survey of Issues and Evidence* (New York: Oxford University Press, 1981), pp. 66-69.

29. Sally Findley, *Planning for Internal Migration: A. Review of Issues and Policies in Developing Countries,* p. 41.

30. Inter-American Development Bank, *Economic and Social Progress in Latin America 1979,* p. 138.

31. W. Arthur Lewis, *The Evolution of the Internanional Economic Order* (Princeton: Princeton University Press, 1978), pp. 39-40.

32. See Johannes F. Linn, "The Costs of Urbanization in Developing Countries", *Economic Development and Cultural Change* 30 (April 1982), pp. 625-648.

33. *Ibid.*

34. Michael P. Todaro, *City Bias and Rural Neglect: The Dilemma of Urban Development* (New York: Population Council, 1981), p. 27.

35. See, for example, Irving Hoch, "Urban Scale and Environmental Quality" in R.G. Ridker (ed.) *Resources and Environmental Implications of United States Population Growth* (Baltimore: Johns Hopkins University Press, 1973); and Inter-American Development Bank, *Economic and Social Progress in Latin America* (Washington, D.C.: IDB, 1979), p. 135.

36. See Bertrand Renaud, *National Urbanization Policy in Developing Countries*, p.7.

37. Harry W. Richardson, "National Urban Development Strategies in Developing Countries", *Urban Studies* 18 (October 1981), p. 272.

38. Michael P. Todaro, "Urbanization in Developing Nations: Trends, Prospects, and Policies", p. 173.

39. See Abdun Noor, *Education and Basic Human Needs* (Washington, D.C.: World Bank Staff Working Paper No. 450, 1981), pp. 2-4.

40. World Bank, *World Development Report 1980* (Washington, D.C.: World Bank, 1980), p. 53.

41. D.C. Rao, "Urban Target Groups" in H. Chenery et al., (eds.) *Redistribution With Growth* (New York: Oxford University Press, 1974), pp. 149-150.

42. *Ibid.*

43. World Bank, *World Development Report 1979* (Washington, D.C.: World Bank, 1979), p. 84.

44. World Bank, *World Development Report 1979*, p. 79.

45. D.C. Rao, "Urban Target Groups", p. 151.

46. John F. Turner, "Uncontrolled Urban Development: Problems and Policies", *International Social Development Review*, No. 1 (1966), pp. 123-124.

47. Julius K. Nyerere, *On Rural Development,* Address to the Food and Agriculture Organization World Conference on Agrarian Reform and Rural Development, Rome, Italy, July 13, 1979, pp. 3-4.

48. P. Coombs and M. Ahmed, *Attacking Rural Poverty: How Non-formal Education Can Help* (Baltimore: Johns Hopkins University Press, 1974), pp. 13-14.

49. Kempe Ronald Hope, "Agriculture and Economic Development in the Caribbean", *Food Policy* 6 (November 1981), p. 253.

50. See David J. King, *Land Reform and Participation of the Rural Poor in the Development Process in African Countries* (Washington, D.C.: World Bank Conference Papers on Land Reform, 1973).

51. Charles Harvey and Others, *Rural Employment and Administration in the Third World: Development Methods   and Alternative Strategies* (Geneva: ILO/Saxon House, 1979), pp. 23-25.

52. See Doreen Warriner,   *Land Reform in Principle   and Practice* (London: Clarendon Press, 1969).

53. Folke Dovring, *Economic Results of Land Reform* (Washington, D.C.: US Agency for International Development, June 1970), p. 23.

54. World Bank, *World Development Report 1982* (New York: Oxford University Press, 1982), p. 84.

55. Bruce F. Johnston and William C. Clark, *Redesigning Rural Development: A Strategic Perspective* (Baltimore: Johns Hopkins University Press, 1982), p. 256.

56. Julius K. Nyerere, *On Rural Development*, p. 8.

57. Denis Goulet, *The Cruel Choice* (New York: Antheneum, 1971), p. 148.

58. Arthur A. Goldsmith and Harvey S. Blustain, *Local Organization and participation in Integrated Rural Development in Jamaica* (Ithaca: Rural Development Committee, Cornell University, 1980), pp. 88-89.

59. William F. Wertheim and Matthias Stiefel, *Production, Equality and Participation in Rural China* (Geneva: UNRISD Participation Programme, 1982), pp. 83-85.

60. Peter Hakim, "Lessons from Grass-Root Development Experience in Latin America and the Caribbean", *Assignment Children*, 59/60, No. 2, (1982), p. 138.

61. See Frances F. Korten, "Community Participation: A Management Perspective on Obstacles and Options" in David C. Korten and Felipe B. Alfonso (eds.) *Bureaucracy and the Poor: Closing the Gap* (West Hartford: Kumarian Press, 1983), pp. 181-200.

62. *Ibid.*

63. This idea and most of the rest of this section is derived from Kempe Ronald Hope, "Development Administration in Post-Independence Guyana", *International Review of Administrative Sciences* 43, No. 1 (1977), pp. 67-72; Kempe Ronald Hope, "Development and Development Administration: Perspectives and Dimensions", *Administrative Change* 7 (July-December 1979), pp. 11-24; Kempe Ronald Hope, "Improving Public Enterprise Management in Developing Countries", *Journal of General Management* 7 (Spring 1982), pp. 72-85; Kempe Ronald Hope, "The Administration of Development in Emergent Nations: The Problems in the Caribbean", *Public Administration and Development* 3 (January 1983), pp. 49-59; Kempe Ronald Hope, "Some Problems of Administering Development in Developing Nations", *Indian Journal of Public Administration* 29 (January-March

1983), pp. 1-10; Kempe Ronald Hope, "The Administration of Development in Developing Nations Revisited", *Public Administration Review* 21 (January-June 1983), pp. 38-62; and Kempe Ronald Hope and Aubrey Armstrong, "Toward the Development of Administrative and Management Capability in Developing Countries", *International Review of Administrative Sciences* 46, No. 4 (1980), pp. 315-321.

2
URBAN POPULATION GROWTH
AND URBANIZATION
IN THE CARIBBEAN

As discussed in Chapter 1, the rapid growth of the urban population and the ensuing urbanization is one of the most significant demographic changes occurring in the Third World today and the Caribbean nations are no exception to this trend. In this chapter the discussion centers on the structure, sources, consequences, and the policy implications of rapid urban population growth and urbanization in the Caribbean.

Structure of Urban Population Growth and Urbanization in the Caribbean

Table 2.1 indicates the rapid pace of urbanization and population growth in the entire Caribbean. Between 1950 and 1970 urban populations in the Caribbean grew at more than twice the rate of the rural populations while during the period 1970 and 1980 the growth rate of the urban population was more than four times that of the rural population and that increasing trend is expected to continue into future.

By the year 2000, it is expected that more than 64 percent of the entire Caribbean's population will reside in urban areas compared to 38 percent in 1960. For the individual countries, Barbados will have 52 percent of its population in the urban areas, while Guyana will have 53 percent, Jamaica will have 79 percent, and Trinidad and Tobago will have 72 percent. This growing rate of urbanization can be further gleaned by looking at the data for the individual countries as shown in Table 2.2.

TABLE 2.1

Average Annual Percent Growth in Urban and Rural Populations
In the Caribbean, 1950-60, 1970-75, 1980-90

URBAN GROWTH RATE			RURAL GROWTH RATE		
1950-60	1970-75	1980-90	1950-60	1970-75	1980-90
2.93	3.31	3.18	1.35	0.73	0.71

SOURCES: United Nations, *Trends and Prospects in Urban and Rural Population, 1950-2000* (New York: United Nations, 1975), Tables C1 and C2; and United Nations, *Patterns of Urban and Rural Population Growth* (New York: United Nations, Population Studies, No. 68, 1980) Annex II.

During the past two decades three of the four Caribbean nations had urban population growth rates exceeding 3.5 percent. In Barbados, the urban population growth was only 1.1 percent. This low growth rate in Barbados reflects the considerable success of the island's family planning program as well as a slower rate of rural-urban migration as will be seen in the next section.

TABLE 2.2

Urban Population as A Percentage of Total Population
and Growth Rates of Urban Population (1960-82),
In the Caribbean

COUNTRY	PERCENTAGE URBAN			GROWTH RATES OF
	1960	1970	1982	URBAN POP. (1960-82)
BARBADOS	40.8	43.5	46.9	1.1
GUYANA	28.9	31.7	49.1	3.8
JAMAICA	34.0	41.6	77.6	7.1
TRINIDAD AND TOBAGO	39.2	53.0	68.1	3.8
CARIBBEAN	38.2	45.1	54.0	

SOURCES: Same as for Table 2.1 ; and Inter-American Development Bank, *Economic and Social Progress in Latin America 1983*(Washington, D.C.: IDB, 1983), p. 346.

Most of the urban population in the Caribbean tend to be located in a single city — the capital city. As the primate city, the capital city contains more than 80 percent of the urban population. By the year 2000 it is estimated that more than 95 percent of the urban population will be located in the capital city and its immediate environs in Barbados and Guyana.[1] It is usually recognized that the concentration of a large percentage of the total urban population in the largest city (primacy) and the existence of a very large urban center in a country are not necessarily found in the same country.[2] However, both factors are true in the Caribbean. Capital cities dominate in the Caribbean for purely historical economic reasons. During the colonial era, the British government felt it necessary to establish all commercial and administrative activities close to the main center of shipping where raw materials were exported and consumer goods imported. And, despite some attempts by the post-colonial governments to influence the population to settle elsewhere, the primate city in the Caribbean remains the focal point of both governmental and private sector activities and, as such, the rational settling place for the population. In Jamaica, for example, Kingston has always been the main destination for rural Jamaicans, and the youth in particular. Indeed, one in four of the population under age 20 live in the Kingston metropolitan area which has 65 percent of the total population of Jamaica.

The urban population in the Caribbean, like the rural population, is predominantly female. The majority of the population is between the ages of 20 to 34. This age peak, of course, coincides with the ages where many studies have shown urbanization to be most rapid.[3] It reflects, in part, the younger accession to the labour force that is typical in urban areas.

Without a doubt an urban bias exists in the Caribbean since the needs of vocal and concentrated urban masses are given preference over the dispersed and less politically aware rural population. But this differential has been a feature of Caribbean society for decades, and the present work focuses on its cumulative effects and what to do about it. At the present time, high concentrations of population in the urban areas of the Caribbean have emerged and are much greater than those found in practically

any other part of the Third World resulting in serious socio-
economic consequences for the individual nations as will be shown
later in this chapter.

Sources of Urban Population Growth and Urbanization in the Caribbean

As documented in the previous section, the rapid growth
of the urban population has led to the uncontrolled urbanization
in the Caribbean. The growth of the urban population results
from two sources, namely, natural population increase and rural-
urban migration. Identifying the relative weight of each source
in the influencing of rapid urbanization is an important first
step in understanding the social and economic processes creating
urban demographic changes. Beyond that, the implications for
policy and planning are also made clear.

Natural Population Increase

In Table 2.3, we see the share of urban growth due to the
natural increase of the population. The data suggests that in
Trinidad and Tobago the natural increase of the urban population
is the primary contributor to urbanization while in Jamaica
that is not the case. For the entire Caribbean region the natural
increase of the population was also found to be responsible for
the bulk of the urban growth.

TABLE 2.3
Natural Population Increase as a Source of Urban Growth, 1970-75
(Percentages)

COUNTRY/REGION	SHARE OF GROWTH DUE TO NATURAL INCREASE
JAMAICA	47.4
TRINIDAD AND TOBAGO	57.9
CARIBBEAN	71.6

SOURCE: Calculated from Bertrand Renaud, *National Urbanization Policy
in Developing Countries* (New York: Oxford University Press, 1981), pp. 165-
166; and Sally Findley, *Planning for Internal Migration: A Review of Issues
and Policies in Developing Countries* (Washington, D.C.: U.S. Government
Printing Office, ISP-RD-4, 1977), p. 36.

The natural increase of any population is determined by the differential between mortality and fertility. That is, the difference between surviving births and deaths. Like the rest of the Third World, the mortality rate in the Caribbean has been declining as seen in Table 2.4. It is anticipated that this trend will continue into the far future as major improvements in life expectancy continue to occur. Currently, life expectancy at birth in the Caribbean region as a whole averages 65 years for both sexes. The average in Barbados is 72 years, in Guyana it is 62 years, in Jamaica it is 72 years and in Trinidad and Tobago it is 71 years. It is believed that the lower life expectancy at birth in Guyana can be attributed to that nation's current economic crisis which in turn has led to a food crisis that has left many families suffering from endemic anemia due to malnutrition.

TABLE 2.4

Crude Death Rate in the Caribbean, 1960-1985
(Per 1,000 Population)

COUNTRY	1960	1970	1980-1985
BARBADOS	12	9	8.4
GUYANA	12	7	5.9
JAMAICA	9	8	6.7
TRINIDAD AND TOBAGO	8	7	6.2

SOURCES: World Bank, *World Tables 1980* (Baltimore: Johns Hopkins University Press, 1980), p. 444; World Bank, *World Development Report 1983* (New York: Oxford University Press, 1983), pp. 186-187; and United Nations, *The World Population Situation in 1983* (New York: United Nations, Population Studies, No. 85, 1984), pp. 103-104.

Additionally, the country's health care system has deteriorated to the point where there is only one physician per 10,000 persons and where medical supplies are virtually unavailable. In all of the countries life expectancy is higher among the female than male sex at birth.

Nevertheless, it is to be expected that negative slopes for the curve of rates of gain in life expectancy will eventually occur during the process of mortality decline. As the more preventable diseases, are successfully controlled, and mortality is determined more and more by diseases of the newborn and of old age as well as by accidental death, the pace of mortality improvement slows. Male mortality has generally been higher than that of females though the reasons for such a phenomenon are not entirely clear cut. In terms of the rural/urban differentials, the data are incomplete but seem to suggest that the rural areas have the lowest life expectancy while the urban areas, which generally concentrate the industries, services, governmental bureaucracy, and better health and living conditions, have the highest life expectancy. Urban and rural mortality differentials are also due to the fact that their populations differ in composition. Urban populations in the Caribbean not only have a more favourable distribution of income but are, on the average, better educated than rural dwellers. Higher levels of education not only equip a mother with the knowledge to provide better care for her children but also, and more importantly, it provides her with the ability to maintain control of her children's care and education rather than having it left to the older family members.

Turning to evidence on fertility in the Caribbean, it can be gleaned from Table 2.5 that the levels of fertility have been declining also reflecting a general demographic transformation. By the end of the century the levels of fertility in Barbados, Guyana,

TABLE 2.5

General Fertility: Births per 1,000 Women 15-49 years old, 1970-2000
(Five Year Annual Agerages)

COUNTRY/ REGION	1970-75	1975-80	1980-85	1985-90	1990-95	1995-2000
BARBADOS	94.9	91.6	85.8	77.0	67.8	60.6
GUYANA	147.3	131.8	113.9	96.9	81.2	69.5
JAMAICA	167.6	149.9	133.3	122.0	110.4	93.5
TRINIDAD & TOBAGO	109.7	95.1	84.5	74.8	68.2	61.9
CARIBBEAN	144.0	137.0	130.5	124.0	115.8	104.8

SOURCE: Inter-American Development Bank, *Economic and Social Progress in Latin America 1980-81* (Washington, D.C.: IDB, 1981), p. 140.

and Trinidad and Tobago will have dropped to levels roughly comparable to those of the. United States and Canada. These projected declines in fertility rates could imply a further increase in the labour force participation of Caribbean women.

Fertility declines in the Caribbean began during the late 1950s and early 1960s as more and more women began to seek higher education and were encouraged to pursue professional careers. However, fertility rates continue to be highest at the younger ages, specifically peaking at ages 20-24, because of low ages at marriage. This is consistent with the general patterns observed in the Third World which indicate that as countries experience declining fertility, reproduction becomes increasingly concentrated in a narrow age range. Fertility rates are also higher in the rural than in the urban areas of the Caribbean as seen in Table 2.6. This is partly explainable by the fact that women in the urban areas tend to be more educated than their rural counterparts and a great many of them are actively working outside of the home which tends to negate childbearing activities. Again, this is consistent with what has been observed in the Third World since the 1960s.

TABLE 2.6

Fertility Differentials in the Caribbean
By Education and Residence*

COUNTRY	EDUCATION			RESIDENCE	
	NONE	PRIMARY	SECONDARY	RURAL	URBAN
GUYANA	5.5	5.1	3.6	5.3	4.1
JAMAICA	—[a]	4.5	2.2	4.8	3.5
TRINIDAD & TOBAGO	—[a]	3.8	2.2	3.9	2.9

SOURCE: Robert Lightbourne, Jr., Susheela Singh, and Cynthia P. Green, "The World Fertility Survey: Charting Global Childbearing", *Population Bulletin 37* (March 1982), p. 22.

*Average Number of Children Ever Born per Ever-Married Woman Aged 30-34.

[a]Less than 20 cases

Despite, the declining fertility of urban women in the Caribbean, fertility remains a most important factor in the natural increase of the urban population and will remain important in the future. As the mortality rate begins to stabilize, it is the rate of births that will determine the actual size of the natural increase. Moreover, estimates of fertility are a necessary component of population policy planning in the Third World, and in particular, the Caribbean where there is a major emphasis on reducing the rates of population growth. In the long-run, however, economic development is the most important way of reducing fertility.

Rural-Urban Migration

In Table 2.7, we see the share of urban growth due to migration for the entire Caribbean region. If the projections and data are correct; it would seem that during the 1980s rural-urban transfers as a percent of urban growth would decline marginally. But a more accurate picture of internal migration as a source of urban growth can be gleaned from Table 2.8 which provides the most recent data on the individual countries.

TABLE 2.7

Average Annual Rate of Rural-Urban Transfers and Rural-Urban Transfers As a percent of Urban Growth in the Caribbean, 1950-60, 1970-75, 1980-90

RURAL -URBAN TRANSFERS PER 1,000 URBAN POPULATION			RURAL-URBAN TRANSFERS AS A PERCENT OF URBAN GROWTH		
1950-60	1970-75	1980-90	1950-60	1970-75	1980-90
5.7	9.4	8.9	19.5	28.4	28.0

SOURCE: Sally Findley, *Planning for Internal Migration: A Review of Issues and Policies in Developing Countries* (Washington, D.C.: Government Printing Office, 1977), p. 36.

Migrants from the rural areas contribute from 42 percent in Trinidad and Tobago to approximately 53 percent in Jamaica, of the annual growth of the urban population in the Caribbean. The vast majority of the migrants are young adults who move to the urban areas for economic betterment. In all of the countries, the majority of the population made at least two major moves.[4] The original move being from a rural to an urban area with subsequent moves to other urban areas. In both Guyana and Trinidad

TABLE 2.8

Internal Migration as a Source of Urban Growth, 1970-75
(percentages)

COUNTRY	URBAN POPULATION GROWTH RATE	SHARE OF GROWTH DUE TO MIGRATION
GUYANA	6.8	51.0
JAMAICA	3.8	52.6
TRINIDAD AND TOBAGO	2.0	42.1

SOURCES: Same as for Table 2.7; and Bertrand Renaud, *National Urbanization Policy in Developing Countries* (New York: Oxford University Press, 1981), pp. 165-166.

and Tobago, the great majority made three moves. Also, with the exception of Guyana, women moved more than men. The greater internal movement of women rather than men can be accounted for, to some extent, by the increasing number of women entering the Caribbean labour force which in turn makes for higher female labour force participation rates.

In the Caribbean, the income earned by migrants in the urban destinations emerges as a most powerful factor influencing the decision to migrate, especially among those with some education, despite the fact that rates of urban unemployment are extremely high. The rural-urban flow is motivated by the expected income differential between the rural agricultural sector and the modern urban sector as well as the expected income differential between the rural sector and the informal urban sector. In Barbados, for example, wages in the rural agricultural sector average approximately 42 percent less than in the non-agricultural sector.[5]

Another variable with a strong positive bearing on rural-urban migration in the Caribbean is that of education. Education influences migration propensity in two primary ways. First, the acquisition of non-farming skills requires settlement in urban areas where there are greater numbers of and better equipped educational institutions. Secondly, the practice of non-farming skills requires settlement in the urban areas where the likelihood of finding a job is much greater despite high rates of un-employment and underemployment.

Perhaps, however, the primary push factor in the rural to urban flow in the Caribbean is the decline in job opportunities caused by a declining agricultural sector.[6] The contribution of the agricultural sector to Gross Domestic Product (GDP) in the Caribbean has been on the decline since the 1960s. Along with the declining share of agriculture in GDP in the Caribbean has been the uneven decline of per capita food production since 1976. Declining per capita food production, apart from indicating the general state of the agricultural sector in the Caribbean, also points out the dilemma of economic development there. One of the fundamental roles that agriculture has to play in economic development is the expansion of local food supplies. This becomes important because as economic development pro-ceeds, there is a substantial increase in the demand for agricultural products.   A failure to expand food supplies might impede economic development, as it results in either an increase in im-ports and loss of foreign reserves or increases in food prices. Spending scarce foreign exchange on food means that less is available to import capital, technology, and other factors of production. Poor agricultural performance, in other words, hinders the growth of the rest of the economy and limits the resources available to promote growth.

The role of agriculture's contribution to employment in the Caribbean is also important here. Since the 1950s the propor-tion of the labour force employed in agriculture has been de-clining. This is due to the structural problems and the trans-formation process currently occurring in that sector. The trans-formation of Caribbean agriculture is consistent with what is expected to occur during economic development. That is, the decreasing importance of the agricultural sector in the national economy and the growing importance of industry and services, primarily as a result of the low income elasticity of demand for agricultural products relative to other products, and of the growing specialization in the Caribbean economy, which shifts workers from the agricultural sector to other dynamic sectors.

Finally, the point must also be made here that expectations about employment and income differentials in Caribbean urban areas are not the only factors which encourage rural-urban

population flows. Expectations about social and cultural amenities, social services, leisure goods, and the quality of life in the
urban areas also play a role in motivating the rural-urban population flow. Although the real income for the migrant families
may not be significantly higher than it was at their place of
origin, their hopes for their future and children's future are
higher and, for this reason, many families continue to be committed to city life.

Consequences of Urban Population Growth and Urbanization in the Caribbean

One of the major consequences of rapid urbanization in the
Caribbean is the buoyant supply of urban job seekers which
has resulted in further increases in the rates of urban unemployment. Though this unemployment issue will be discussed in
greater detail in the next chapter suffice to say here that the
urban economy in the Caribbean, through to its current evolution,
has not been able to generate enough economic activity to absorb
the growing numbers of the urban labour force. It is in this context of slowly growing urban employment opportunities accompanied by a disproportionately high rate of rural-urban migration
that the chronic urban unemployment and underemployment
problems have emerged in the Caribbean. Rapid urbanization
in excess of job opportunities is therefore both a symptom of
and a contributing factor to the slow rate of urban economic
growth in the Caribbean. The numerical size and rate of growth
of the urban population is excessive in relationship to the absorptive capacity of the urban areas. That is, the urban economy
lacks the ability to productively employ growing numbers of new
labour force entrants. Yet − because development is geared to
the urban economies with the resultant effects of severe imbalances in job opportunities and wage scales, and an education
system geared toward urban residents − rural residents in the
Caribbean assume that their economic future can only be secured
by moving to the cities to seek their fortunes despite their narrow
chances of success.

A further consequence of rapid urban population growth
and urbanization in the Caribbean which results from rural-urban
transfers is that of the fertility factor. The vast majority of Caribbean migrants tend to be in the peak reproductive age groups.

They are young adults whose fertility is higher than that of the urban population as a whole. They are concentrated in the 15-30 age range and are primarily women. Their departure from the rural areas not only reduces the size of the rural population directly but has the potential of an even greater effect because the children born to them are likely to go with them and future births will also occur in the urban destinations. This raises the issue of the migration "demographic multiplier". There is a migration demographic-multiplier because migrants are generally young, under 30, and move to the urban areas during their most fertile years. The effect of the demographic multiplier is longer-lasting than those of the employment multiplier. Its magnitude is related to patterns of family formation and is rather country-specific.[7] Furthermore, the effects of the demographic multiplier guarantee that the population of the urban areas will continue to grow naturally by large absolute numbers for quite a while. This in turn guarantees further upward pressure on the absorptive capacity of the urban areas. That is, the ability of the urban economy and society to productively employ growing numbers of new labour force entrants and to provide basic public services to accomodate them.

Urban public services are unable to keep pace with the demand in the Caribbean. Hospitals and schools are overcrowded in the urban centers. Major traffic congestion occurs during most of the working hours indicating a high degree of motorization in the primate cities. Indeed, it has been found that the degree of motorization is associated with the level of income of a country and a city.[8] In Kingston, Jamaica, for example, only 16 percent of all work trips (25 percent of school trips) are made on foot, and less than one percent on bicycles.[9] In Trinidad and Tobago, traffic congestion is greater in the urban centers not only because there are more cars per capita, but also because transport problems are more complex there. Housing, already too expensive for the majority of urban dwellers, is becoming almost unavailable and squatter settlements are becoming prevalent. Crowding within the dwelling and the neighborhood is more severe in the poorest of the urban areas. In West Kingston, for example, over 90 percent of the dwellings are in various states of dilapidation. The same is true for Albouystown in Guyana. In examining the distribution of tenure arrangements in urban areas, between owner occupancy, rental, and other forms of tenure, it is found that in both Jamaica and Trinidad and Tobago more than 60 percent of the conventional dwellings are rented. The importance of urban housing in the Caribbean is further demonstrated by the substantial portions of households' budgets that are spent on such housing. On average, households spend between 20 and 30 percent of their total expenditure on urban housing in the Caribbean compared to the average of between 15 to 25 percent in the Third World.[10] This clearly demonstrates the extent to which urban housing demand exceeds supply in the Caribbean and thereby creating an inflated housing market. To cope with this situation many urban residents, particularly migrants, live in small, multi-family residences giving rise to tremendous overcrowding and unsanitary conditions. This combination of overcrowding and poor housing is generally accompanied by a low level of services. These residences and the communities in which they are located tend to lack potable water, proper drainage, sewerage, and electrical facilities.

Of tremendous importance here also is the changing social fabric of the urban centers. Urban violence and crime, for example, have become widespread. Such activities are largely perpetrated by the unemployed. And, indeed there seems to be a direct correlation between high rates of urban unemployment and high rates of urban crime. In Guyana, for example, recent data indicate a crime rate of 179 per 10,000 population in the urban areas as opposed to a rate of 59 and 97 per 10,000 population in the rural areas and nationally, respectively.[11] In Trinidad and Tobago, the homicide rate per 100,000 inhabitants was found to be 15.3 in the primate city (Port-of-Spain) compared to a national rate of 14.0 during the 1966-70 period.[12] However, in contrast to violent crime, property crime as well as victimless crime appears to be more common in the urban than rural areas. This differentiation can be attributed to the greater opportunities for burglary and robbery in the urban areas than in the rural areas. In the rural areas, residents are known to each other and family members tend to be at home tending to the residence. In the urban areas, family members are likely to be away from home during the business hours pursuing education or fulfilling their employment obligations.

In the Caribbean, urban food supplies which once came from the rural areas now have to be imported due to the declining agricultural sector which, in turn, has resulted in declining per capita food production. People who live in urban areas cannot live off the land. As such, access to food supplies is now determined by financial resources. The four countries in this study together currently spend a little more than US$420 million on the importation of food each year. The composition of the import bill for the Caribbean nations gives an indication of the major food deficiencies of the region. The most important imported items are animal proteins — meat, dairy and fish products — which make up more than 50 percent of the total value of food imports, while fruits and vegetables account for about 8 percent. In terms of intraregional trade of agricultural products, Barbados and Guyana are responsible for approximately 30 percent of the imports, while Guyana and Trinidad and Tobago are responsible for approximately 40 percent of the exports. The regional integration effort in the Caribbean has hardly affected agriculture. This is so primarily because agricultural exports from the Caribbean go to destinations outside the region rather than to other countries within it. Moreover, the countries of the region generally have similar weather, topography, and soils, leading to a high degree of intraregional competition rather than to complementarity in the crops produced.[13] As such, increasingly, the agricultural surplus that feeds the urban areas comes not from the surrounding countryside but from abroad. Reliance on imported food has thus increased with urbanization. Such reliance on faraway food supplies is expensive in the short-run and economically disastrous in the long-run. Moreover, the financial inability to meet demand, as is currently the case in Guyana, leads to inadequate diets and malnutrition. Malnutrition, in turn, causes both mental and physical retardation, and poor diets also affect general health.

The social and economic consequences of rapid urban population growth and urbanization are interdependent. In the Caribbean, there is no clear line dividing social from economic factors. However, social consequences are defined here as changes in the network, pattern, and attitude toward social relationships. These may include changes in the roles within the family structure and relations, patterns of informal social contacts, and even the pattern of participation in formal associations. For the rural-urban migrants the most dramatic social changes are those involved in shifting from a rural to an urban lifestyle. The majority of the migrants for reasons of insecurity, their lack of familiarity with the cities, and the expense of locating and acquiring housing, reside with their relatives or close friends and this condemns them to accept the established norms and customs of that household.

However, apart from that adjustment, migrants who reside with relatives or friends tend to be better off than those who do not. Those without kin or friends to help them are at a severe disadvantage in finding jobs and building adequate lives for themselves. Whereas, friends and kin in the urban areas facilitate migrant adjustment to the urban areas by providing loans of cash or kind to tide the migrants over until they find their own source of income; by helping them become involved in the city's social life, easing the transition from rural to urban customs; and, perhaps most importantly, help the migrants find jobs. Also of importance here is the role changes of female migrants in the Caribbean. Caribbean women have generally been regarded as subordinate and of secondary importance to men.[14] However, as migrants, they are predominatly single; they tend to be between the ages of 15 and 30; and they tend to have an average of two dependents. These factors necessitate the need for them to seek employment and better incomes in the urban areas and, in that respect, the reasons for departing from the rural areas are similar to those of Caribbean men. But even in cases where women are married, they may also have to work for additional income to supply family necessities previously derived from farming or relatives.

Caribbean migrants also maintain significant ties with their rural areas of origin and with people of common origin. Frequent contact with the rural areas and a sense of belonging to the village home carry over to several generations. Migrants return home for regular visits and remittances — the flow of funds back into the rural village - are sent back at regular intervals. These remittances are not only an effective means of redistributing incomes from the urban to the rural areas but also are important to the improvement of the condition of the rural families who receive them. A great many rural families in the Caribbean depend on these remittances for their subsistence. These remittances are used primarily to purchase consumer and household goods while from the more affluent migrants and their families remittances may also be used to maintain homes, land, and other property owned in the rural areas. However, there is one significant disadvantage of remittances. This is, they tend to hamper other development processes. Because remittances go to parents or other family members, it becomes possible for the recipients to increase their consumption without changing their economic system or habits. This results in a loss in pressure for change and the rural areas may be less able to develop.

In addition to the social and economic consequences there are also some political consequences of rapid urbanization. Political activity, like most other activities in the Caribbean, is centered around the urban areas. As such, and except during national election campaigns, rural residents tend to show little interest in issues of politics. Rural migrants therefore exhibit no desire to get involved in urban politics during their initial period of residence in the urban areas. In other words, they attempt to remain politically aloof.[15] However, they soon find themselves actively involved having been influenced by their friends and relatives. In the Caribbean, this influence is transmitted and reinforced through the racial and ethnic cleavages that exist. The migrant soon realizes that some type of political affiliation is necessary in the urban areas and that it is useful that such affiliation be along racial and/or ethnic lines. As such, the rural-urban migrants, having been recruited and influenced, quietly adapt to urban political behaviour. They become in earnest, participants in the political process with representative membership in institutionalized political groupings that can be mobilized or tapped for political support by astute politicians.

Conclusions and Policy Implications

Rapid urban population growth and urbanization seem entrenched in the Caribbean. Along with such growth comes the social, economic, and political consequences discussed in the foregoing section. The Caribbean has been found to be characterized by acute inequality of income between the urban and rural populations and between different categories of workers and socio-economic classes, with a chronically high level of urban unemployment and rural underemployment. The declining agricultural sector as well as the implementation of development strategies with an urban bias have resulted in rapid rural-urban migration which is almost equally responisble for the growing Caribbean urbainzation which, in turn, is responsible for the serious socio-economic dislocations occurring in the urban centers of the Caribbean.

But, although continued and even accelerated rural-urban migration seems inevitable in the Caribbean, there has been a tendency to do very little about it. This has tended to create distortions and imbalances in both economic and social opportunities between the rural and urban areas. However, any concern with socio-economic development must focus attention on the relationship between the migration/employment dilemma and development. This means the discouraging of rural-urban migration through policies which emphasize the development of the rural sector in the Caribbean. Yet, there is very little information on the relationship of migration to rural development or on the relationship of policy to migration. Most of the effort has been concentrated on family planning programs. That is, on fertility control. However, any complete evaluation of the dynamics of population change, of the interrelation between population and development, and of potential policies for coping with problem conditions in urban and rural locations cannot rest on attention to one component of population change alone (fertility) but must focus as well on the other major component (migration) and on the interaction between both.

The fertility factor will, however, remain important in the Caribbean. Interrelations between migration and fertility are complex and relate both to whether those leaving rural areas have higher or lower fertility than those remaining behind; whether, in turn, rural to urban migrants differ in their fertility behaviour from the natives of the cities; and whether the migrants are in fact contributing more than their share of children to the natural population increase of the urban areas.

Solving the problems associated with rapid urban population growth and attempting to diffuse urbanization in the Caribbean must entail the placing of central emphasis on the creation of urban employment opportunities. The problem of urban unemployment in the Caribbean is in reality a range of related problems, some more serious, some less serious, most extending well beyond the groups directly affected by open unemployment.

While the urban population growth causes increases in the labour force and rural-urban migration continues, there is an immediate need for expanded employment opportunities and a viable population planning policy.

The low absorption capacity of the urbanized manufacturing sector in the Caribbean is particularly striking in this regard because the reduction of the agricultural labour force has been accompanied not only by very high rates of unemployment but also by a substantial reduction, by 12 percent, of the ratio of employment to working-age population.[16] Women and young people are mainly affected by this unemployment.

What is needed then, are integrated appropriate national urbanization policies for the individual Caribbean nations. The integrated urbanization strategy combines the integrated rural development approach with an explicit focus on developing rural service centers, market towns, and small cities. Instead of focusing soley on rural development, this strategy recognizes that rural development is linked to a network of central places serving rural areas. The smaller secondary cities and market towns serve rural development needs, improving rural employment and reducing rural outmigration.[17]

This type of urbanization policy lies in creating industrialization from the ground up simultaneously with investments in agriculture. It is, in other words, a policy of complementarity between the rural and urban sectors and directed at diversification of the entire economy. However, its progress must stay in balance and the benefits must be shared reasonably between the two sectors. In the past, the distribution of the benefits associated with modernization has been constantly directed toward the urban areas and, rural residents, quite sensibly, flocked to them. If, however, rural incomes approximate parity with urban ones, the element of economic coercion in rural-urban migration will be largely removed. If rural standards of living can be generally raised then the rural exodus can be stemmed. The growth of the urban population in the Caribbean will not, however, cease. But with a concerned retreat from urban bias and a serious commitment to complementary urban and rural development, urban population growth and urbanization could proceed in a manageable manner.

Notes

1. See United Nations, *Patterns of Urban and Rural Population Growth* (New York: United Nations, Population Studies No. 68, 1980), pp. 128-131.

2. Bertrand Renaud, *National Urbanization Policy in Developing Countries* (New York: Oxford University Press, 1981), p. 107.

3. See, for example, Lorene Y.L. Yap, "The Attraction of Cities: A Review of the Migration Literature", *Journal of Development Economics* 4 (September 1977), pp. 239-264.

4. Kempe Ronald Hope and Terry Ruefli, "Rural-Urban Migration and the Development Process: A Caribbean Case Study", *Labour and Society* 6 (April-June 1981), pp. 141-148.

5. *Ibid.,* p. 144.

6. See Kempe Ronald Hope, "Agriculture and the Urbanization Process in the Caribbean", *Regional Development Dialogue,* Special Issue Edited by Benjamin Higgins (Nagoya, Japan: United Nations Center for Regional Development, 1982), pp. 65-78.

7. Bertrand Renaud, *National Urbanization Policy in Developing Countries,* p. 88.

8. Johannes F. Linn, *Cities in the Developing World: Policies for Their Equitable and Efficient Growth* (New York: Oxford University Press, 1983), p. 91.

9. Government of Jamaica, Ministry of Finance and Planning, *Urban Growth and Management Study: Interim Report No. 3* (Kingston: National Planning Agency, 1978), p. 2.12.

10. Johannes F. Linn, *Cities in the Developing World: Policies for Their Equitable and Efficient Growth,* p. 120.

11. Howard Jones, *Crime, Race and Culture: A Study in a Developing Country* (New York: John Wiley and Sons, 1981), pp. 42-44.

12. Alan Gilbert and Josef Gugler, *Cities, Poverty, and Development: Urbanization in the Third World* (New York: Oxford University Press, 1982), p. 126.

13. Kempe Ronald Hope, "Agriculture and Economic Development in the Caribbean", *Food Policy* 6 (November 1981), pp. 258-259.

14. See Frances Henry and Pamela Wilson, "The Status of Women in Caribbean Societies: An Overview of their Social, Economic and Sexual Roles", *Social and Economic Studies* 24 (June 1975), pp. 165-198.

15. Joan Nelson, *Access to Power: Politics and the Urban Poor in Developing Nations* (Princeton: Princeton University Press, 1979), pp. 112-116.

16. International Labour Office, *Growth, Employment and Basic Needs in Latin America and the Caribbean* (Geneva: International Labour Office, 1979), p. 34.

17. See Kempe Ronald Hope, "Urban Population Growth in the Caribbean", *Cities* 1 (November 1983), pp. 167-174.

3

UNEMPLOYMENT, LABOUR FORCE PARTICIPATION, AND URBANIZATION IN THE CARIBBEAN

The single most important influence on urban concentration has been the nature and location of employment. Both migrants and individuals born in the urban areas are required to find subsistance, but the speed with which they initiate this search, the intensity with which they conduct it, and the eventual outcome, differs between age groups and ethnic groups, and by level of education and other factors.[1]

The availability of jobs is, arguably, the most important element in the quality of urban life. Perhaps too much of the debate about the urban condition focuses on the supply of services such as piped water, transportation, housing, and education. Although provision of these services can vastly improve the well-being of the urban poor, it does not solve their basic problem which is poverty. Productive employment does.[2] This chapter examines the primary issues related to unemployment and labour force participation within the context of Caribbean urbanization.

The Extent of Unemployment in the Caribbean

It is a mere tautology, and it has been shown in this work also, that the level of urban unemployment, or rather urban underemployment, is due to the difference between the rate of growth of the active population in urban centers and that of the employment opportunities created there. This is true for the rural areas also. However, like most of the Third World, the problem is of major significance in the urban areas of the Caribbean because of its greater visibility due to hidden unemployment in the rural areas. But, since hidden unemployment and under-employment are not usually included in the official unemployment data, the urban unemployment rate tends to be understated particularly during prolonged recessionary periods when the number of discouraged workers tends to increase.

In Table 3.1 we see the national unemployment rates for the Caribbean. In Barbados, the period from 1970 to 1980 witnessed an 18 percent increase in the labour force, largely due to a substantial rise in the female participation rate and population increase. Consequently, although employment expanded over the period, the overall unemployment rate jumped from 9 percent in 1970 to 13.7 percent in 1980. In Guyana, the unemployment rate increased from roughly 16 percent in 1970 to an estimated 20 percent in 1980. Guyana's labour force in 1980 was 34 percent of the total population. A partial factor giving rise to Jamaica's record unemployment rates is the curtailment of imports which occurred in the 1970s and which in turn provoked acute shortages of raw materials and intermediate goods, thereby further reducing the level of economic activity in the manufacturing, construction, and distributive trade sectors. At present, the situation is further compounded by the lack of foreign exchange to import raw materials. In Trinidad and Tobago, where there is still a vibrant private sector, the 1980 unemployment rate was 8.7 percent.

TABLE 3.1

National Unemployment Rates in the Caribbean, 1960-80
(Percent)

COUNTRY	1960	1970	1980
BARBADOS	8.0	9.0	13.7
GUYANA	8.0	16.0	20.0[a]
JAMAICA	13.0	18.0	27.3
TRINIDAD AND TOBAGO	12.0	12.5	8.7

SOURCES: World Bank, *World Tables 1976* (Baltimore: Johns Hopkins University Press, 1976), pp. 514-517; Inter-American Development Bank, *Economic and Social Progress in Latin America* (Washington, D.C.: IDB, Several Years); and Caribbean Development Bank, *Annual Report 1982* (St. Michael, Barbados: CDB, 1983), p. 24.

[a]estimate.

More recent data indicates that by the end of 1983 the unemployment rate was 16 percent in Barbados, 32 percent in Guyana, 28 percent in Jamaica, and 14 percent in Trinidad and Tobago.

In Table 3.2 we see the data on urban and rural unemployment rates that is currently available. Information on urban unemployment in the Caribbean is difficult to obtain. For some reason such data tend not be developed in the country censuses. Moreover, when such data are developed their accuracy are highly questionable due to the qualitative differences in the census questionaires and differences in the definitions of urban areas. However, despite those limitations it is clear that urban unemployment rates exceed by far the rural unemployment rates. In Jamaica the ratio of urban to rural unemployment rates is 1.5, for Trinidad and Tobago it is 1.9 while for Guyana it is 1.3.

TABLE 3.2
Urban and Rural Unemployment Rates in the Caribbean
(Percent)

COUNTRY	YEAR	UNEMPLOYMENT RATE	
		URBAN	RURAL
GUYANA	1965	20.5[a]	15.4[c]
JAMAICA	1960	19.0[a]	12.4[b]
TRINIDAD AND TOBAGO	1971	16.5	8.7

SOURCES: David Turnham and I. Jaeger, *The Employment Problem in Less Developed Countries: A Review of Evidence* (Paris: OECD, 1971), pp. 57; 134-135; and Lyn Squire, *Employment Policy in Developing Countries; A Survey of Issues and Evidence* (New York: Oxford University Press,1981),p.68.

[a]capital city only   [b]excluding capital city   [c]estimate.

But, despite how unemployment is calculated, it is at too high a level in the Caribbean nations, and is increasing rapidly perhaps with the exception of Trinidad and Tobago where there still exists a vibrant private sector and where economic growth rates, though not spectacular, have been steady. As demonstrated above, much of the increase is in the urban centers, where high rates of open unemployment are added to the more typical underemployment in both the urban and rural areas. The conversion of rural underemployment into open unemployment in urban centers changes both the magnitude and the political nature of the problem. But despite the large and increasing un-employment of unskilled labour in the urban areas, there is a simultaneous shortage of high-level professionals. This is the case because of the considerable emigration of high-level personnel from the Caribbean. The incidence of emigration among high-level manpower from Trinidad and Tobago is currently averaging 15 percent. Annual emigration of professional, technical, and management personnel from Jamaica represents roughly 10 percent of the incremental growth of manpower in that nation. In Guyana, the magnitude of emigration is much greater. There, high-level personnel constitute about 25 percent of the permanent emigrants per year. In Barbados, similar patterns prevail.[3]

In general, rapid rural-urban migration is more significant in explaining the magnitude of the urban unemployment problem than the rate of industrial job-creation. Industrial job creation is increasing at a rate that is far from high enough to absorb migration from rural areas. In some of the countries, such as Guyana, the rate of industrial job-creation has even been negative. However, at the base of the problem lies the too-rapid growth of the labour force flowing from high population growth rates over-all.

Age and Sex Composition

One of the main characteristics of urban unemployment in the Third World is that the proportion of the young people who are affected is generally large. In nearly every case, including the Caribbean, the unemployment rates in the 15-24 age group are disproportionately high. The most recent data estimate that the rate for that age group in Guyana is 40 percent while in Trinidad and Tobago it is 26 percent. Similarly, females have lower work rates and higher rates of unemployment. Barbados shows appreciably higher work rates than other countries while for the primary work force groups of males ages 25 to 29 years, Jamaica and Trinidad and Tobago show unusually low work rates.[4]

The general problem of manpower utilization in the Carib-bean, as measured by work rate data, is highly concentrated among females and the younger members of the working age population. Approximately 80 percent of the non-working po-tential labour force did not want a job, a vast majority being females engaged in housekeeping.[5] This therefore suggests that the actual socioeconomic costs of the unemployment problem tend to be far more serous in the case of younger males. The composition of those who were said to have wanted work tended to be highly concentrated among those seeking their first job. The youngest age group (14 to 19 years old) accounted for approximately half of all work seekers in the Caribbean region. There were roughly twice as many males as females in both the 14 to 19 and the 19 and over age groups.[6] The region is therefore faced with the perennial probelm of providing employment for young workers. That is, the problem of absorbing young school leavers into the economic life of the countries.

Educational Levels

Although the data on educational levels are not abundant, they are sufficient for valid conclusions to be drawn from them. Unemployment is much more of a problem for those individuals having moderate educational qualifications. The most recent available data for Trinidad and Tobago, for example, suggests that the unemployment rate was about 10 percent of the labour force for those with less than 5 years of education, and about 6 percent for those with a completed secondary school education or higher.[7]

Education in the Caribbean is a much sought after commodity and its pursuit a very competitive activity. In many of the countries, such as Guyana, education is encouraged and provided universally through to the university degree. In such an environment, then, academic achievement tends to set individuals apart, particularly as it relates to the hiring process since it becomes a primary factor in the process of staff determination. In the urban areas of the Caribbean the significance of education to the employment, or the lack of employment, situation is more entrenched because both the acquisition and practice of skills usually require residency in the urban areas.

Patterns of Labour Force Participation in the Caribbean

Unquestionably then, rapid urbanization is the primary factor influencing urban unemployment in the Caribbean. Given the rates of internal migration and the natural population increase in the urban areas, it is not surprising that urban unemployment has emerged as a serious problem in the Caribbean. When unemployment and underemployment in the Caribbean persists it means a loss of productive activity for the economy as a whole, but to the unemployed it means a loss of income, less food, poor shelter, less of all the basic elements needed to satisfy human needs, and a general perpetuation of their state of poverty.[8] This hopeless economic situation in turn can and has resulted in unmanagable social problems such as high crime rates in Jamaica and Guyana,[9] for example, as discussed in the preceeding Chapter.

In all of the Caribbean nations, the rate of unemployment is higher than in the United States and other industrial countries at any time in this century including the depression. Thus, the problem of unemployment is on the one hand a sterile statistic used by economists, but on the other hand, to millions of Caribbean citizens it signifies frustration, idleness, and poverty.[10] Within that context the growth, composition, and pattern of labour force participation becomes significant.

Size, Growth, and Sex Composition of the Labour Force

As seen in Table 3.3, during the period 1960-2000 the labour force in the Caribbean is expected to grow two-fold in absolute terms. At present, the labour force in the Caribbean is estimated at about 30 percent of the total population. The number of workers in the labour force is dependent on both the pool of existing workers and those entering the labour force. The growth rate is contigent upon population increase, net migration, and social and economic factors. The two primary socio-economic factors are education and socialization. In terms of education there is a strong correlation between increased education and increased labour force participation for both men and women. Socialization dictates an individual's perception of his or her role in society and this affects the decision on whether to enter the labour force. As economies expand, for example, there is a decrease in the labour force participation of children since parents feel education is a much more important alternative; on the other hand, there is an increase in the participation of women since they seek financial benefits instead of staying at home. These two factors are interrelated. For example, since more and more Caribbean women are seeking higher education and entering the labour force not only could their fertility rate tend to decline in the future but also the population growth rate could fall.

TABLE 3.3

Caribbean Labour Force, 1960-2000

(Thousands)

COUNTRY	1960	1965	1970	1975	1980	1985	1990	1995	2000
BARBADOS	91	89	90	98	107	115	125	133	143
GUYANA	173	187	204	242	288	341	391	442	493
JAMAICA	608	630	636	672	749	858	966	1071	1171
TRINIDAD & TOBAGO	281	285	314	354	403	453	495	533	568
TOTAL	1153	1191	1244	1366	1547	1767	1977	2179	2375

SOURCE: International Labour Office, *Labour Force Estimates and Projections 1950-2000* (Geneva: ILO, 1977).

In examining the growth rates of the total labour force in each of the four nations as well as its male and female components, as shown in Table 3.4, several conclusions can be drawn, all of which have implications for urban unemployment. First, in the decade and half preceding 1970, the growth of the total labour force in each country was modest and, with the exception of Guyana, all of the countries had periods of negative growth. Second, with the exception of Jamaica, the rate of growth of the female sex in the labour force was greater than that of the male sex after 1970. This reflects a trend which is becoming more pronounced, namely, the increase of women in the labour force. Even though their total number has remained relatively small in comparison to men, the increase has been enough to influence the average growth of the labour force as a whole.

Sectoral Composition of the Labour Force

The sectoral distribution of the labour force is shown in Table 3.5. As can be seen, the patterns of change of sectoral activity of the labour force between 1960 and 1980 has been quite similar. During the past twenty years important shifts have occurred in the sectors in which work is sought. Whereas in 1960, a large number were in agriculture, by 1980 the majority of workers were employed in industry and services with the services sector having the highest proportion. It is clear therefore that the shift taking place in the labour force is away from agriculture and into services as the primary sector in the Caribbean.

TABLE 3.4

Average Annual Rates of Growth of Caribbean Labour Force By Sex,1955-2000
(Percentages)

PERIOD	BARBADOS			GUYANA			JAMAICA			TRINIDAD & TOBAGO		
	TOTAL	MALE	FEMALE	TOTAL	MALE	FEMALE	TOTAL	MALE	FEMALE	TOTAL	MALE	FEMALE
1955-60	-1.30	-1.29	-1.30	1.09	1.39	0.13	-1.05	-1.45	-0.35	2.33	2.12	2.93
1960-65	-0.55	-0.18	-1.06	1.57	1.40	2.13	0.72	0.44	1.19	0.34	-0.59	2.72
1965-70	0.31	0.65	-0.20	1.73	1.61	2.12	0.18	-0.10	0.64	1.92	2.07	1.58
1970-75	1.67	1.63	1.74	3.48	3.29	4.08	1.10	1.27	0.83	2.41	2.28	2.72
1975-80	1.81	1.80	1.81	3.50	3.29	4.12	2.21	2.31	2.05	2.63	2.45	3.04
1980-85	1.44	1.51	1.33	3.45	3.24	4.06	2.75	2.67	2.88	2.37	2.18	2.78
1985-90	1.58	1.57	1.59	2.91	2.72	3.47	2.48	2.45	2.53	1.87	1.68	2.29
1990-95	1.41	1.39	1.44	2.68	2.52	3.10	2.27	2.18	2.43	1.60	1.41	2.00
1995-2000	1.43	1.32	1.60	2.48	2.27	3.03	2.07	1.94	2.27	1.38	1.16	1.81

SOURCE: Same as for Table 3.3

While the proportion involved in agriculture in the Caribbean continues to be considerably higher than in the more developed countries of the world, the numbers in the services sector are rapidly approaching those of the more developed countries.

TABLE 3.5

Sectoral Composition of Caribbean Labour Force,
1960, 1970, 1980
(Percentages)

SECTOR	BARBADOS			GUYANA			JAMAICA			TRINIDAD & TOBAGO		
	1960	1970	1980	1960	1970	1980	1960	1970	1980	1960	1970	1980
AGRICUL-TURE	26	20	9	34	28	31^a	39	29	21	22	19	16
INDUSTRY	27	32	26^a	29	33	33^a	25	26	25	34	35	36
SERVICES	47	48	65^a	37	39	36^a	36	45	54	44	46	48

SOURCES: World Bank, *World Tables 1980* (Baltimore: Johns Hopkins University Press, 1980), pp. 462-463; World Bank, *World Development Report 1982* (New York: Oxford University Press, 1982), pp. 146-147; and Inter-American Development Bank, *Economic and Social Progress in Latin America* (Washington, D.C.: IDB, Several Years).

[a] most recent estimate

The major difference has been that only about one-third of the workers in the Caribbean are in industry whereas in the developed nations it is almost twice that percantage. However, when comparing the Caribbean to Africa and Asia it was found that in the latter two regions agricultural activities have tended to dominate the sectoral composition of the labour force by a wide margin.

The growth in labour force activity in the services sector has been accompanied by another trend in the evolution of the economies of the Caribbean. The growth of service sector employment has occurred together with the urban population explosion and the growth of women in the labour force. The services sector is the main sector absorbing women in the labour force. This may be hapenning at a quicker pace than the growth in the women's labour force because the service sector has grown at the expense of agriculture and industry since the late 1950s. Though the rapid growth of services sector activity is a new phenomenon in the Caribbean economy, it can be stated that one of the reasons the supply of labour has shifted from agriculture to the services and industry sectors has been the greater opportunities for employment in that modern sector which is located exclusively in the urban areas. The declining share of agriculture in total employment is a reasonable quantitative index of the degree and evolution of urbanization.

It is obvious then that the structural changes occurring in the sectoral composition of the Caribbean labour force are a major contributor to the rapid urbanization occurring in the Caribbean. The services sector (of which the major employer is the government) and the industry sector are found in the urban centers usually in one major city which is always, in the case of the Caribbean, the capital city. This type of urban primacy is mirrored in the urban-size distribution by the way one city dominates all the others.[11] As such, Kingston, Jamaica, has twelve times the population of Montego Bay, for example.

Moreover, such urban primacy has led to the creation of organized labour markets in the urban areas. The organized labour markets comprise virtually all public sector jobs and that part of the private sector in which conditions of employment are subject to some degree of collective bargining. They account for between thirty and fifty percent of total employment, and wages and related benefits tend to be somewhat better than in the unorganized labour market.[12]

However, how effectively and efficiently the service and industry sectors can continue to absorb such a large influx of workers remains to be seen. This, of course, will be dependent on the extent to which the traditional agricultural sector is left behind the more modern industrial and service sectors. Since the modern sector is often characterized by relatively higher wage rates, there is usually a supply of labour available to this sector. Therefore, the growth of employment in the modern sector is primarily determined by the growth in the demand for labour.[13]

Participation Rates of the Labour Force

In Table 3.6 the participation rates of the Caribbean labour force are exhibited for 1970 and 1975. The trends in participation rates were not substantially different from that obtained in other regions. The major difference is that, until recently, the number of women entering the labour force of the Caribbean countries was small. Currently, the female labour force participation rate in the Caribbean region is approximately 19.5 percent and is lower than that obtaining in most of Asia, Western Africa, and Eastern Africa.

TABLE 3.6

Caribbean Labour Force Participation Rates By Sex,
1970 and 1975
(Percentages)

| COUNTRY/REGION | 1970 | | | 1975 | | |
	TOTAL	MEN	WOMEN	TOTAL	MEN	WOMEN
BARBADOS	40.5	48.7	32.4	40.0	50.3	30.6
GUYANA	30.1	46.5	13.7	30.6	46.3	15.0
JAMAICA	32.2	42.1	22.7	33.1	41.2	25.2
TRINIDAD & TOBAGO	33.1	48.1	18.5	35.1	49.0	21.2
CARIBBEAN	33.5	46.0	21.3	35.3	50.4	19.5

SOURCES: Same as for Table 3.3; and Norma Abdulah, *The Labour Force in the Commonwealth Caribbean:A Statistical Analysis* (St. Augustine,Trinidad: Institute of Social and Economic Research, University of the West Indies, 1977), p.13.

Where country differences in participation rates exist, they are only partially due to differences in the age and sex composition of the populations. The differences narrow down in the case of males when the rates are standardized for differences in age distribution, but actually increase in the case of females. Thus, the relatively low female participation rate in Guyana can be explained by the age composition of the population. About 55 percent of Guyana's population is below the age of twenty. However, the relatively high female participation rates of Barbados cannot be attributed to the island's particular age structure. Although, as would be expected, the chief differences in age- and sex - specific participation rates are found among the relatively younger and older ages, they are also plainly present among workers in the intermediate age groups.[14]

In general, participation rates tend to be significantly lower among the younger age groups of the working population than those of older workers. Similarly, females typically have lower participation rates than males of corresponding age. Differences in age-and sex-specific participation rates in the Caribbean region conform to this general pattern, but the relative magnitudes of the differences appear to be atypically large.[15] Perhaps the most visible change occurring with respect to labour force participation rates in the Caribbean, and hence influencing economic life, is the rapid entrance of women into the work force. As Table 3.4 shows, the female labour force in the four countries will continue to outgrow the male labour force into the year 2000 and there is no reason to believe that this expansionary trend will not continue past the turn of the century. The number of women working or seeking jobs in the four countries as a whole will grow at an annual rate of 2.5 percent between 1975 and the end of the century while the rate for men will be 2 percent.

Another significant aspect of this phenomenon is that while the labour force participation rate for women as a whole, is rising, importantly, that of the younger age group is increasing faster and, even more importantly, is the proportion of women living and working in urban areas. For all the countries, women outnumber men in urban areas as shown in the previous chapter. Recent partial analyses suggest that female urban labour force growth is even higher than had been projected. However, a more precise judgement will require the evidence which will be available after all the countries complete the computation of the data from the 1980 censuses and when various international organizations such as the United Nations and the International Labour Office have had an opportunity to recalculate the forecasts. This whole process usually takes 4-7 years after the census is completed

This urban orientation of the female population of the Caribbean can be further gleaned from data on the sectoral distribution of the female labour force as discussed in the previous section. Carrbbean women working in the non-agricultural activities by far outnumbered working women in the agricultural sector. In Jamaica, for example, 82 percent of the women in the labour force have jobs or are seeking jobs in the non-agricultural sector. Working women in the Caribbean were twice as likely to hold a white-collar job as men. For the four countries as a whole, 27.6 percent of the working women had white-collar jobs compared to 12.8 percent of working men. However, there are some striking differences within each country. For example, 36.8 percent of working women in Trinidad and Tobago had a white-collar job, compared with only 23.4 percent of working women in Jamaica.[16] Clearly, opportunities exist for women to obtain good jobs. They are provided with the same opportunity as men to prepare themsleves and acquire the necessary skills and training and there is a strong correlation between women's increased educational opportunities and higher female labour force participation rates.

Another very important aspect in the issue of female labour force participation is the increasing number of female-headed households which is a growing phenomenon in the Caribbean. In the Commonwealth Caribbean, 35 percent of all heads of households are women.[17] For women who are heads of households, the most viable way of securing an income and hence safeguarding their families, is to enter the labour force.

The above discussion of labour force participation, therefore, points to the changing economic and social dynamics of the roles of women in the Caribbean particularly as it influences the process of rapid urbanization. This will have a profound effect on regional economic development in the future especially since the consequences of these changes have yet to be incorporated into the institutional, social, and economic structures in the Caribbean.

Policy Implications and Conclusions

As far back as 1933 Allan Fisher espoused a stage theory of development that touted the rising significance of the services sector as economic devleopment proceeds.[18] A little more than two decades later Colin Clarke elaborated essentially the same idea on the dynamics of labour force composition by arguing that as time goes on and economic development occurs, the number of workers in the agricultural sector tends to decline relative to the number in manufacturing, which in turn decline relative to the numbers employed in the services sector.[19] These two frameworks become known in the literature as the "Clarke-Fisher hypothesis" and remain valid even more so today than before.

In the Caribbean, the same pattern has been observed. As the agricultural sector declined with the passing of time and the movement toward modernization took hold, all of the major occupational groups became more highly urbanized. In the case of industry and services, this tendency reinforced a pre-existing urban dominance in the primate capital city. As a result, after the labour force growth began to exceed the rate of urban job expansion, urban unemployment became a major dilemma.

Perhaps the primary concern with the urban unemployment problem in the Caribbean is that it includes a pool of persons who, because they are not employed, are not contributing to their own well-being and the gross national output.[20] This does not only result in socio-economic problems for the urban unemployed but it also influences unsuccessful job-seekers to abandon their search thus creating a cadre of discouraged job-seekers and further reducing the national productivity effort. Moreover, the concentrated incidence of unemployment on such a politically vocal and influential group makes this an especially pressing social issue in the Caribbean and it must be corrected urgently.

When persistent unemployment causes individuals to drop out of the labour force they cease to be counted as unemployed. Thus, as useful as the unemployment rate may be, it does not represent a full picture of the labour market. Low participation rates may be an indication of the presence of discouraged workers, and a signal that labour market conditions may well be worse than the rate of unemployment indicates. In the Caribbean, participation rates by age, sex, and ethnicity provide an insight into labour market conditions that the unemployment rates alone does not give. These insights can be very useful in the planning of remedial action.

Caribbean policy-makers seem to have regarded rapid urbanization as an irresistible force of nature and have done very little to manage it. As such, policies to guarantee a steady growth of jobs which also allow for economic expansion in all sectors, both in the intermediate and long term, are almost non-existent. However, the reduction of urban unemployment must be given some priority in the development plans of the Caribbean nations. A reduction of urban unemployment must be made through a slowing down of the process of urban population growth and urbanization, which in turn also implies a slowing down of rural-urban migration as well as through attempts to increase the demand for labour.

A solution to the urban employment problem would be difficult enough if it were just a matter of jobs. However, the kinds of jobs, the increases in output, and other factors are all important if the labour force is to be productive. Caribbean families depend on their jobs for income to buy the necessities for their families. The continued growth of urban unemployment will exacerbate this already acute problem.

The expansion of urban job opportunities is not a naturally occurring phenomenon. The problem exists now and will remain until the end of the century, at least. Increasing the number of jobs now would, of course, help raise income but the problem will reoccur unless there is a continued effort to expand employment opportunities in order to match the steady growth of the labour force. The growth of output which is necessary to absorb such large numbers of workers may not be attainable for some countries. However, by not even trying to expand employment opportunities, the Caribbean governments may foredoom millions more to poverty.

Notes

1. Stuart W. Sinclair, *Urbanization and Labour Markets in Developing Countries* (New York: St. Martin's Press, 1978), p. 69.

2. Kathleen Newland, *City Limits: Emerging Constraints on Urban Growth* (Washington, D.C.: Worldwatch Institute, 1980), p. 20.

3. See Kempe Ronald Hope, "The Emigration of High-Level Manpower from Developing to Developed Countries With Reference to Trinidad and Tobago", *International Migration* 14, No. 3 (1976), pp. 209-218; James Sackey, "The Migration of High-Level Personnel from Guyana: Toward an Alternative Analysis", *Transition* 1, No. 1 (1978), pp. 45-58; and G. Ebanks, P.M. George and C.E. Nobbe, "Emigration From Barbados, 1951-1970", *Social and Economic Studies* 28 (June 1979), pp. 431-449.

4. Sidney E. Chernick and Others, The *Commonwealth Caribbean: The Integration Experience* (Baltimore: Johns Hopkins University Press, 1978), p. 74.

5. Jack Harewood, *Unemployment and Related Problems in the Commonwealth Caribbean* (St. Augustine, Trinidad: Institute of Social and Economic Research, University of the West Indies, 1978), p. 28.

6. Sidney E. Chernick and Others, *The Commonwealth Caribbean: The Integration Experience*, p. 75. For a slightly varied interpretation of the data see Norma Abdulah, *The Labour Force in the Commonwealth Caribbean: A Statistical Analysis* (St. Augustine: Institute of Social and Economic Research, University of the West Indies, 1977), pp. 59-63.

7. Jack Harewood, *Unemployment and Related Problems in the Commonwealth Caribbean*, p. 29.

8. See Kempe Ronald Hope, "A Note on the Unemployment Problem in the Caribbean", *Labour and Society* 8 (July-September 1983), pp. 271-276.

9. See Howard Jones, *Crime, Race and Culture: A Study in a Developing Country* (New York: John Wiley and Sons, 1981), pp. 150-156; and Klaus De Albuquerque and Others, "Uncontrolled Urbanization in the Developing World: A Jamaican Case Study", *Journal of Developing Areas* 14 (April 1980), p. 365.

10. See Kempe Ronald Hope, "The Employment Problem, Rural-Urban Migration and Urbanization in the Caribbean", *Population Review* 26, Nos. 1 and 2 (1982), p. 42.

11. Alan Gilbert and Josef Gugler, *Cities, Poverty, and Development* (New York: Oxford University Press, 1982), p. 30.

12. Sidney E. Chernick and Others, *The Commonwealth Caribbean: The Integration Experience*, pp. 81-82.

13. A.S. Oberai, *Changes in the Structure of Employment With Economic Development* (Geneva: International Labour Office, 1978), p. 20.

14. Sidney E. Chernick and Others, *The Commonwealth Caribbean: The International Experience*, p. 66.

15. *Ibid.*, p. 74.

16. *Ibid.*, p. 76.

17. See Mayra Buvinic, *Women Workers in Latin America: A Structural Analysis* (Washington, D.C.: International Center for Research on Women, May 1981).

18. Allan G.B. Fisher, "Capital and the Growth of Knowledge" *Economic Journal* (1933), pp. 374-389.

19. Colin Clarke, *The Conditions of Economic Progress* (London: MacMillan and Company, 1957), p. 492.

20. Jack Harewood, *Unemployment and Related Problems in the Commonwealth Caribbean*, pp. 56-57.

4

TOWARD POLICIES
FOR MANAGING RAPID
URBANIZATION IN THE CARIBBEAN

This book has shown that urban population growth and rapid urbanization have significant negative effects on the citizens and economies of the countries in the Caribbean. These negative effects fall into three categories. First, in all of the countries the concentration of people in urban areas clearly does not bring about an optimal distribution of resources. The process of economic development would proceed at a much faster and stable rate if urbanization were controlled. Secondly, the quality of life in the urban areas of the Caribbean is rapidly declining. Poverty is rampant, basic needs are not being met, and anti-social manifestations have become more frequent. The third category pertains to the widening differential between the urban and rural areas. On the one hand, an urban bias has led to modernization and the potential for higher living standards in the urban centers while, on the other hand, neglect of rural areas has resulted in the maintenance of a traditional and poverty-stricken rural economy. This urban-rural dichotomy has been described as the most important class conflict in the poor countries of the world today.[1] Moreover, as long as this urban bias exists in the Caribbean, urbanization will continue to be a pressing problem there.

This chapter delineates the dynamics of a set of rural development, urban development, and population policies necessary to manage urban population growth and urbanization in the Caribbean. The policies advocated here should be applicable, perhaps with some modifications, with equal success in each of the countries because they are basically similar in terms of their economic and social structure as well as their patterns of urbanization. Policies designed to manage rapid urbanization must necessarily be integrated in nature and directed at bringing about both rural and urban development through a total national effort, as well as a reduction in the rate of population growth.

Rural Development Policies

In Chapter One, rural development was defined not simply as agricultural and economic growth but as a far-reaching transformation of social and economic institutions, structures, relationships, and processes in rural areas. It was also argued that for rural development to be successful it must be integrated in nature. The integrated rural development strategy focuses most heavily on the agricultural sector and attempts to retain people in or move them into rural areas. Developed mass agriculture is normally needed before it is possible to have widespread successful growth in other sectors.[2]   Such rural development strategies require vigorous government actions, the understanding and active collaboration of the private sector, and a general mobilization of the people to help solve the crucial problem of rural poverty. From the purely national aspect, it is essential that rural development be carried out within the framework of overall economic and social policy.

As industrialization was pursued in the Caribbean, the role of the rural sector was neglected. However, rural development cannot any longer be conceived as being separate from industrial development and other sectors of the economy. Neither is it possible to think that great industrial development will induce agriculture to expand automatically. It is true that industrialization creates urban markets for some agricultural products. It has been seen, however, that due to the Caribbean's urban growth, industrialization alone has not been capable of usefully absorbing the expanding labour force. The interrelation between both sectors is very close, and adequate planning must exist in developing both. Furthermore, in the past the foreign exchange earnings from the agricultural sector permitted the expansion of industrial output and employment in the Caribbean and can certainly do so again in the future.

Agricultural Policy

The major issues in agricultural development in the Caribbean are how to sustain a rate of growth that allows for a balanced expansion of all parts of the economy, and how to ensure that the pattern of agricultural growth will make a strong and direct impact on rural poverty and will reduce migration of rural residents to urban areas. Agricultural development in the Caribbean seems to suffer from basic problems associated with the structure of the industry, and technical and institutional weaknesses. But, the overall decline and transformation of Caribbean agriculture seems consistent with what was expected to occur: that is, the agricultural sector has become less important in the national economy and industry and the service sectors have become more important. However, it is desirable that this decline be accompanied by increased productivity and food production capacity to supply the growing share of the population not employed in agriculture. This process has to take place in the very near future since the relatively low productivity of agriculture has given rise to another severe problem, namely, the problem of feeding the expanding population of the Caribbean over the long-term. Accelerated growth in agricultural production not only increases each nation's chances of feeding its population but it also can sharply increase the transfer of resources between agriculture and other sectors of the economy. Such changes affect relative rates of capital formation and income growth in various sectors, the structure of growth, and overall rates of growth.

Sustained agricultural production, however, requires major policy decisions and some steps have been taken in that direction. A Regional Food Plan (RFP) was designed by the Caribbean governments and was approved in 1975. The RFP was designed specifically to reduce the region's rapidly rising food import bill through the implementation of projects to supply the region with vital agricultural inputs. Food imports in the region now exceed US$600 million per year (of which more than 70 percent is attributable to the four countries in this study) and have been expanding annually even in volume terms. Additionally, a Caribbean Food Corporation (CFC) was established in 1976 as the primary regional institution for implementing the RFP. The CFC is concerned with all stages of agricultural production and distribution.

It will, in cooperation with national agencies, identify, plan and implement projects. It will finance and undertake such projects on a joint basis with the public and private sector or on its own. Additionally, Jamaica established its own Emergency Production Plan which had as its primary goal the restructuring of the agricultural sector.

The CFC grew out of efforts towards implementing an improved trade regime in the agricultural sector through the establishment of joint regional projects. Some marginal progress has been made with respect to the RFP but its implementation has moved slowly because Caribbean agricultural development has historically been geared to the production of traditional export crops. As a result, the infrastructure and institutional underpinnings required for increased production of domestic foodstuffs are either inadequate or non-existent. Although the CFC, the implementing agency for the RFP, was established in 1976, it required time to move it from a formal act of "creation" to an operational institution with full capacity to perform its designated functions and it was not until 1979 that some of the Caribbean governments took legislative action to give the CFC an operational status. By 1980 the CFC was fully operational and was working on approximately 25 projects which were included in its investment program through 1984-85.

However, the Caribbean governments need to place renewed emphasis and interest in the RFP, and the CFC must be allowed to secure the necessary financial and managerial resources to proceed with its mandate. Such projects as the Rhynesbury Regional Project, located in Jamaica, under which agriculturists are to be trained as middle-level farm managers for national and regional projects, must continue to be encouraged and implemented. Moreover, the CFC ought to ensure that it does not duplicate the efforts of private sector agricultural production and thus waste its scarce resources.

In any attempt at increasing agricultural production, consideration must be given to two factors. First, increasing the acreage available for agricultural production; and second, increasing the crop yield. In the first case, the issue is one of expanding cropped area through new land development. Jamaica, for example, had made some progress in that direction in the

1970s when land was made available to small farmers under Project Land Lease and Project Self-Help. More recently, in 1983 to be exact, the government of Jamaica launched a bold new program, called AGRO 21, as a new thrust in agriculture to put unused and under-used land to work to create employment and earn more foreign exchange. But, with the exception of Guyana where there are government-owned and controlled estates, land holdings in the Caribbean have taken the form either of large estates involved in commercial, export-oriented agriculture, or small owner-operated farms. In both cases significant inefficiences result.

On the large estates inefficiencies in land use occur primarily because of the land volume which remains uncultivated. Estates usually cultivate one crop on the most suitable sections of their total holding so that while output per acre of cultivated lands might be high, output per acre of land owned is typically much lower. Moreover, the particular crop that is usually produced for export trends to be related to the needs of the parent company and is not necessarily the most appropriate crop for the land. Estates are also plagued by a chronic shortage of labour. This is caused by three factors: the social stigma attached to plantation work; the high wages paid to the small section of the labour force working in modern capital-intensive activities; and, the comparatively more strenuous nature of agricultural work.[3]

On the small farms inefficiencies exist because of poor cultivation practices; poor and inadequate use of inputs such as fertilizer; the absence of proper soil conservation and irrigation methods; and the sporadic provision of complementary services. The combined effect of all these factors is that small land-holders are one of the poorest groups in the region.

Land reform, therefore, seems necessary in the Caribbean. With the exception of Guyana, the land reform effort in the Caribbean has been marginal. Jamaica, for example, has experimented with State farms and cooperatives but none of those programs has been successful. It is, therefore, necessary that a major program of land reform be implemented in the Caribbean.

Land reform embraces the position that small is beautiful. Contrary to preconceived ideas, many studies have shown that small farms typically use more labour per unit of land than large farms. Since the more intensive application of labour is also associated with higher yields, achieving a more equitable distribution of land ownership offers the prospect not only of improving rural equity, but also of increasing output and labour demand.[4] Rural small-scale farming has therefore demonstrated a remarkable capacity to respond to increases in demand and to provide jobs for rural labour — both of which benefits the Caribbean must strive for.

Land transfer to the small farmers in the Caribbean will bring about an increase in their income which is likely to remain in the rural areas. Under such circumstances, the savings of the small farmers are likely to increase and, as such, increase the capital pool in the rural areas. An increased capital pool in turn would lead to the availability of funds for further rural investment or for ploughing back into the existing farms.

Related to the issue of agricultural productivity and income, resulting from land reform, is the dependence of small farmers on infrastructure, extension services, and research activities that will induce and maintain increased efficiency in food production. However, all of these factors are grossly inadequate in the Caribbean. In 1974, the Caribbean Agricultural Research and Development Institute (CARDI) was established. Concurrently, the Caribbean Agricultural and Rural Development Advisory Training Service (CARDATS) was established. Both institutions were established for the purposes of determining and transferring technology to the small farmer. But both institutions have been terribly ineffective to date, primarily because of the lack of financial support they currently receive from member governments. At the same time, international financial support exerts considerable leverage on the direction of the research and technology application programs. Not only do donors approve the proposed research programs, but they also support technical experts and equipment which influence the style as well as the outcomes of the research programs which are not always in the best interests of the Caribbean nation.[5] Of course, this needs to be changed if agricultural research and training in the Caribbean are going to contribute to increased agricultural productivity and development. Specifically, attention has to be directed to budgeting scarce resources (financial and personnel) toward those projects of immediate importance for technological improvement at the rural community level.

A fundamental problem affecting agricultural activity in the Caribbean is that of the lack of adequate agricultural credit. Some marginal steps have been taken, at the institutional level, to alleviate the problem in recent times. Guyana, for example, has established two cooperative banks. One of them, the Guyana National Cooperative Bank (GNCB), was established in 1970 primarily to mobilize the savings of the nation and to act as the government's financial agent in the promotion and financing of all types of cooperatives. The GNCB is a fully fledged commercial bank operating on sound development banking principles.[6] The second bank created was the Guyana Agricultural Cooperative Bank (GACB). The main purpose of the GACB is that of mobilizing the savings and the financing of agricultural cooperatives and other rural development projects. In Jamaica, there is the Jamaica Development Bank (JDB) which is responsible for the financing of the agricultural sector, among other sectors, and in Trinidad and Tobago there is the Agricultural Development Bank which provides agricultural credit at subsidized rates to both commercial and small-scale farming. Additionally, the Caribbean Development Bank (CDB) has been attempting to finance agricultural projects, primarily in the smaller Least Developed Caribbean Countries (LDCC's) with the assistance of such international organizations as the International Fund for Agricultural Development (IFAD).

However, despite the fact that the lending volume of these institutions has increased in recent years, the overall magnitude of agricultural credit is still limited in the Caribbean. A primary issue seems to be unequal access.[7] It was found, that, in Guyana, for example, the major constraint in the use of credit came from inadequate demand which was the result of the low incomes and backwardness of the farmers.[8] This, therefore, means that access to credit must be equalized. Also of importance here is the fact that adequate monitoring and evaluations must take place, when credit is approved, to reduce the likelihood of default. Though, it has been found that loans to small-scale borrowers are not necessarily more risky, as has been shown in India, Kenya and Lebanon. In fact there is no inverse correlation between the size of a loan and the degree of risk, and the proportion of bad and doubtful debts is not higher among small bank customers.[9] However, should riskiness be a problem, collective guarantee arrangements for rural loans can be used and coupled with crop insurance to eliminate the need for other collateral in the Caribbean.

An agricultural credit system in the Caribbean must allow free transfer of resources between sectors, between regions, and across income classes to bring about an efficient allocation of a country's scarce resources. It must finance the needs arising from the use of appropriate technology in agriculture. It must encourage and mobilize savings from the incomes generated by the expanding agricultural production. As an important factor of production, credit must play a pivotal role in fostering an equitable distribution of the increasing agricultural income.[10] The extent to which agricultural credit can perform these various diverse functions effectively rests, on the one hand, on the national commitment of the Caribbean governments and, on the other hand, on the organizational abilities and skilled human resources required to create and nurture an appropriate institutional infrastructure.

Agricultural credit policies in the Caribbean must aim at eliminating distortions which discriminate against a fuller absorption of manpower in agriculture. Moreover, the problem of over-centralization of the various credit programs must be dealt with. Any organization delivering credit to farmers, especially where the loans are small, as in the Caribbean, has to be widely dispersed, well adapted to local conditions, and be free of red tape. Studies of farmer attitudes have shown that farmers often feel so negatively about the red tape and delays inherent in centralized programs that they prefer to borrow from the local money lenders who can operate more quickly and flexibly, even though charging higher interest rates[11] and thereby increasing the risk to the borrowers.

Ideally, what is needed in the Caribbean is the development and extension of financial institutions into the rural areas. Such organized rural money markets may influence households' savings behaviour in several ways.[12] On the one hand, they may augment the household's liquidity pool through credit. The additional liquidity allows rural households to maintain consumption which would otherwise be disturbed by uneven income flows. Credit further allows households to make major purchases of consumer durables and large productive capital goods. On the other hand, organized rural money markets may provide households with additional savings-investment activities by offering various types of financial savings instruments. If these instruments provide positive real returns to the households, they may induce the households to convert some of their excess liquidity into financial savings. This may increase the average rate of return realized by the households on their savings portfolio and induce the households to divert more of their income to savings-instrument activities by offering various types of financial savings instruments.

Another relevant issue in any discussion on agricultural policy in the Caribbean is that of marketing. No production plan, agricultural or otherwise, can be effective without assured markets. It seems to be much easier to produce than to distribute production in the Caribbean. All of the countries in this study do have or have had national marketing boards. It is clear however that these agencies have not been very effective. Both the Agricultural Marketing Protocol (AMP) and the Guaranteed Marketing Scheme (GMS) within the Caribbean Common Market (CARICOM) framework must be improved, particularly with respect to pricing policy which at the present time emphasizes production costs rather than market circumstances. Profitable prices are a strong incentive to production. Therefore, production and marketing programs should also include an adequate policy of price maintenance.

The goal of the marketing system in the Caribbean must be that of performing the reciprocal function of providing an outlet for producers and food for consumers (households and processing firms). The system must operate to move a variety of farm and food products to consumers in the desired forms and conditions, and to deliver them at prices people are willing and able to pay. Secondly, the marketing system has an allocative function that goes beyond the exchange transactions between farmers and consumers. The marketing system has an influence on the allocation of resources also: on the amount and types of credit made available to the agricultural sector; the research policies that should be pursued and for which crops; the facilities that should be provided in terms of technology; and so on.[13] As such, agricultural marketing in the Caribbean must also be regarded as a significant function in both the determination of, and meeting, the needs of farmers with respect to both inputs and outputs.

The importance of the agricultural sector and its contribution to economic development in the Caribbean cannot be over-emphasized, despite the structural problems that currently exist. Caribbean governments must reverse the decline in agricultural output and reduce their dependence on food imports. The fore-going considerations indicate the need for introducing institutional reforms and structural changes to increase agricultural production while at the same time expanding employment in the sector to reduce the consideration of migration to the urban centers. Promoting agricultural growth and encouraging the efficient use of rural labour are the most important means of reducing rural unemployment and underemployment in the Caribbean.

Rural Nonagricultural Activities

Rural development projects that contribute to the broadly based growth of agriculture provide considerable indirect support for the growth of rural nonagricultural activities be affecting the growth of rural markets for nonfood goods and services. An increasing share of the rural labour force is performing nonfarm work. The increase is partly a result of the slow growth of employment in agriculture as well as the increasing division of labour in rural areas between agricultural and nonagricultural work in the Caribbean. The majority of rural nonagricultural projects are in the form of public works programs. These programs tend to be labour-intensive and they have emerged as important instruments for use in alleviating rural unemployment and underemployment. Though data on the expenditures associated with such projects in the Caribbean are scarce, research observation indicates that most of the expenditure is directed toward maintenance of existing infrastructure rather than the creation of new infrastructure. Moreover, that expenditure appears to be minimal.

However, given the employment and other direct as well as indirect benefits of such projects,[14] their identification and funding must become more concentrated in the Caribbean. At a fairly general level, it has been demonstrated that more jobs and higher incomes for poorly paid rural workers result from an expansion of rural nonagricultural activities.[15] Since such activities seem to combine all those elements necessary for spreading the benefits of development to lower-income groups through growth in employment and wages, they deserve close attention in the formulation of development policies that emphasize rural development in the Caribbean.

Included in non-agricultural activities also is the provision of basic public services. Such public services as: health care, potable water, educational facilities, electricity, insect control, proper roads and transportation networks, and access to non-agricultural goods and services are all taken for granted in the urban centers. However, they are woefully inadequate in the rural areas and must be beefed up if indeed the urban-rural gap is to be diminished. Admittedly, Caribbean governments are not yet in a position to duplicate some of the aforementioned services in the rural areas, due to the cost factor, but basic needs have to be met. Health care centers, potable and frequently running water, and consistently available electricity need to be given urgent attention in Guyana, Jamaica, and Trinidad and Tobago where those problems seem to be more pressing than in Barbados. The benefits of providing such rural public services are essential for improvements in the living standards of Caribbean rural residents which in turn will have a tremendous influence on their retention in the rural communities.

Something should also be said about the role of the private sector here. Except in Guyana — where government activity accounts for more than 80 percent of all economic activity — private sector activity is vehemently encouraged in all of the countries in this study. Such encouragement ought to be extended to pursuade private entrepreneurs to invest in the rural areas where both land and labour are cheaper. Such private rural investment is lacking in the Caribbean for the now all too familiar reasons generated in this study and elsewhere. The problem, as Michael Lipton points out, is not a lack of available self-interested course of action by urban firms to benefit the rural sector, but rather the problem is that the gains from pressing for urban-biased policies are more familiar, rapid, short-term, and therefore cumulative.[16] The private sector must therefore be provided with incentives that would encourage their participation in the rural sector.

Participation of the Rural Population

There is now a large body of literature that indicates that agricultural projects often do not meet their goals because they fail to involve the rural population in the planning and implementation of the projects.[17] Participation in some sense, therefore, seems necessary for successful development efforts. It must be regarded not only as a way of satisfying essential needs but also as a basic need in itself whenever it allows for fuller integration of the various groups in a country's social structure and contributes to bringing about a more egalitarian society from the point of view of distribution of power.[18] Development efforts need local support to succeed, and this is most likely to be forthcoming if project beneficiaries are consulted about their needs, given assistance that meets those needs, and provided with opportunities to influence project decisions.[19]

In the Caribbean, some steady efforts have been made toward participation of the rural population in rural development programs. In Jamaica, for example, participation of local organizations has been stressed in the integrated rural development projects, through the various branches of the Jamaica Agricultural Society (JAS), in the project areas.[20] In Guyana, such participation has been encouraged through the cooperative movement and local councils. Such participatory efforts must continue to be developed as more rural development projects come on stream in the future. Moreover, such participation must not be allowed to succumb to the influence of the urban bureaucracy which is remote from its immediate social environments, separated by culture and "evolution" from its rural cousins, rarely seen by villagers, and indifferent to the needs of its citizen-clients.[21] As such, a rural administrative structure that provides for a direct line of command from the local participants to the field levels must be established in order to ensure that policy is enforced and supported at all levels. This is in essence administrative decentralization designed to bring about decision-making to levels closer to the people.

Despite what the urban-based Caribbean governments and bureaucracy may think, the rural population know what they require to satisfy their interests, meet their needs, and solve their problems. The local population is the depository of the traditional empirical knowledge — including, besides the environment and concrete technological solutions, the socio-economic and cultural characteristics of the community — which can only be transmitted through an active interchange between scientists and the local people.[22] However, this does not mean that the local population is aware of all the obstacles that are likely to come to the fore or will avoid serious mistakes and pitfalls. Mistakes will be made and failures will occur, but if the people affected are in charge and have access to needed technical assistance and training, they are likely to learn and emerge stronger for the next challenge.[23] Such was the recent experience in Jamaica in the Second Integrated Rural Development Project. [24] Capacity-building training was provided to the beneficiaries to help them expand their demand for the services offered; to develop their own capacity to identify problems and solutions; and to work cooperatively to implement the solutions generated.

The success of any participatory program in the Caribbean, however, depends on the continued and committed support of the political leadership. Economic activity of any kind cannot be initiated unless sanctioned at the official political level. In other words, nothing gets done without the proper consultation and blessing of the political apparatus. Such is the nature of the organization of life in the Caribbean. Rural participation there-fore requires political decisions. It cannot be spontaneous in societies like the Caribbean where the rural masses have always been objectively and subjectively dependent on urban elitist rule. It has to be steered by a committed leadership for its success to be guaranteed since it involves matters relating to the redistribution of power. Such a redistribution of power, however, has a tendency to be resisted since it also involves an erosion of the authority of the centralized urban bureaucracy. Such resistance, however, must not be allowed to suppress the participatory initiative — an initiative that has tremendous advantages not only to the rural sectors but indirectly to the individual nations as a whole.

Urban Development Policies

Even if, due to rural development, rural-urban migration were to end miraculously overnight, the urban areas of the Caribbean would have solved only about one-half of the problem of rapid urbanization. The natural increase of urban populations would continue unimpeded and the consequences of urbanization would still be detrimental. Moreover, urban growth will continue even if policy biases favouring urbanization are eliminated and vigorous decentralization measures are deployed. Modern industrial and service activities benefit from the economies of agglomeration, and to the extent that industrialization and structural change are necessary for economic development, the impetus for urbanization will prevail. As such, government policies cannot simply be limited to control of urban population growth. Policies must also be concerned with overall urban development, particularly the improvement of urban public services and the implementation of a viable industrial policy.

Urban Public Services

Urban public services are in a state of disarray in the Caribbean. Though, from the point of view of the rural population, urban residents are much better off in terms of their access to public services and social amenities, urban public services are in a progressive state of deterioration in the Caribbean. Potable water and electricity tend to be frequently unavailable without prior notice; transport services are inadequate mainly due to the inability to purchase spare parts for proper maintenance; telephones routinely do not work; hospitals are pitifully understaffed; a number of schools are overcrowded; and so on. This state of affairs has a disproportionate negative impact on the poor who are not in a position to seek out and obtain alternative services. The problems of deteriorating urban public services are not all due to the inability of Caribbean governments to finance them adequately. Rather, a great deal of the problem has to do with mismanagement and neglect. In Guyana, for example, priority has been shifted to national security expenditure. Clearly, however, to neglect urban services is to invite social upheaval from a population that is bound to become disgruntled sooner or later as evidenced in Jamaica where various community residents frequently block the roads in Kingston to protest the deteriorating state of the same roads and the infrequent supply of water. Moreover, if urbanization is to be properly managed in the Caribbean then the existing urban population must be accommodated.

Specifically, planning for urban development needs to be implemented in the Caribbean. Such urban planning must place central emphasis on the fact that the primate city is also the capital city and that services often matter more than housing because they cannot be provided by self-help, especially for the poor. Moreover, if industrialization is to proceed, so that employment can be provided, then the basic urban infrastructure must also be in place as a positive influence on the investment decision. It would not be possible to encourage private investment if such things as transportation, electrical power, potable water, and so on, are inadequate. Also, and more ideally if resources permit, attempts to decongest the primate cities must continue. Industrial parks on the outskirts of cities need to be designated. New housing schemes must also be promoted beyond city boundaries. In other words, secondary cities, perhaps incorporating suburban areas, must be developed. Secondary city strategies give equal attention to social infrastructure and industrial infrastructure, rather than being biased in favour of the latter.[25] This suggests a stronger orientation to welfare and equity considerations, than is the case with the primate city strategies, while at the same time stimulating economic development.

Secondary cities in the Caribbean can provide the socio-economic impetus needed to generate productive non-agricultural employment by building their capacity to provide services, facilities, and markets for agricultural products and to begin absorbing the surplus labour from both the rural and urban areas. The problems of urbanization and rural-urban migration in the Caribbean cannot be dealt with effectively through rural development alone. As such, the option of developing secondary cities must be given high priority there. Secondary cities can perform a number of additional functions of significant benefit to the Caribbean population. Included are convenient locations for the decentralizing of public services thereby creating greater access for both urban and rural residents to public goods and facilities; they can absorb large numbers of rural-urban migrants thereby creating a more balanced distribution of the urban population and reducing the pressures on the primate city; they can act as the central points of integration of the urban areas and rural economies; and they can act as intermediate centers of marketing and the distribution of both agricultural and non-agricultural products.

Industrial Policy

Industrial policy in the Caribbean must aim not only at the generation of employment but also at creating a permanent industrial base that would encourage complementary or ancillary industries. An industrial strategy that focuses on employment must begin by recognizing the existence of surplus labor and then determine how this labor can be absorbed in the context of both the organized and informal sectors since the urban unemployment problem cannot be solved by relying on only the expansion of the organized sector. Instead of ignoring the informal sector, or actively discriminating against it as in the past, governmental efforts must allow the urban informal sector to gain access to more productive resources. Policies must emphasize the redirecting of some investment to the informal sector to provide education, training, access to credit, and public services that might increase the productive output and income-earning opportunities of the working poor in that sector.

For the organized sector, industrialization cannot be geared to the home markets because of their small size. As such, the only feasible industrialization strategy in small countries with limited natural resources, like those discussed in this book, lies in the creation of export-oriented industries or services.[26] Given such limited natural resources, the Caribbean countries have two primary areas of economic activity where this export-led growth has been attempted, and will have to continue to be attempted in the future, namely, tourism and manufacturing.

With the exception of Guyana, tourism is of vital importance to the economies of the Caribbean nations. It has contributed significantly to foreign exchange, national income, and, being labour-intensive, to the generation of employment. In 1983, tourist expenditures totalled US$252 million in Barbados, US$4.2 million in Guyana, US$409.6 million in Jamaica, and US$225.0 million in Trinidad and Tobago. These tourist expenditures have provided the Caribbean nations with a major portion of their foreign exchange earnings and represents the most conspicuous benefit of tourism. Tourist related activities contribute an average of 20 percent of Jamaica's foreign exchange earnings and about 4 percent of GDP while in Barbados such activities generate slightly more than 19 percent of GDP and 42 percent of good and non-factor service export earnings. The employment contribution of tourism varies considerably in the Caribbean. A total of more than 2,400 people are employed in Trinidad and Tobago, slightly more than 4,000 in Barbados, and over 9,500 in Jamaica's tourist industry. Two categories of people appear to benefit particularly from the employment opportunities provided by tourism in the Caribbean. These are young people and women. But, despite the fact that the Caribbean tourism sector has provided many jobs for women and those jobs have had liberating effects, the burden of seasonal employment in the tourist industry seems to be borne by female employees. That means that during the low season more women are likely to be laid off than men.[27]

There is no doubt that tourism has a major positive impact on the economies of the Caribbean nations and can continue to do so if the sector is carefully planned and regulated. Unlike other industries, however, the tourism product is consumed at the point of production and brings the consumer into direct contact with the producer. In order, therefore, to minimise possible negative social aspects while at the same time maximising the likely benefits, the tourism industry must be under regular governmental scrutiny and appraisal. In particular, there must be integration of tourism planning with the rest of the economy and more local control of the marketing of the industry to ensure greater exposure of the tourism product in its many facets. In this regard, the Caribbean Tourism Research and Development Centre (CTRC) and the Caribbean Tourism Association (CTA), respectively, should be allowed to play major roles. Additionally, hotel and tourism management training should be expanded to cover all aspects of the industry while at the same time ensuring a supply of skilled individuals to run the industry.

The performance of the manufacturing sector in the Caribbean has been erratic. The manufacturing industry's share of GDP has changed unevenly during the last two decades. It increased considerably in some years and likewise declined in some years. The generally similar economic characteristics of the countries has led to a broadly similar pattern of industrialization, although the timing and extent of industrial development has varied. The manufacturing sector's value added in Barbados was 12.3 percent of GDP in 1983, 13 percent in Guyana, 16 percent in Jamaica, and 10.5 percent in Trinidad and Tobago. These four countries account for approximately 94 percent of manufacturing gross domestic product of the CARICOM region. Manufacturing in the Caribbean tends to depend heavily on imported inputs. On the whole, the local value added is small and few linkages have been generated within the domestic economy. The obvious

reason for this state of affairs is that few raw materials and intermediate industries exist locally. The small size of domestic
markets inhibits the establishment of intermediate manufacturing,
which, to be efficient, needs to operate on a reasonably large scale.
Size also affects the sector's ability to contribute to the employment of the growing Caribbean labour force. Available data on
manufacturing exports, as an indicator of export volume, indicate
that during the period 1976-78 all four of the countries had
negative mean annual growth rates (-5.2 percent in Barbados;
-12.4 percent in Guyana; -12.6 percent in Jamaica; and -4.8
percent in Trinidad and Tobago). For the same period only
Barbados had positive mean annual growth rates in the foreign
exchange earnings of manufacturing exports. Barbados's rate of
growth was 27.7 percent, in Jamaica it was -8.8 percent, in
Guyana it was -9.3 percent, and in Trinidad and Tobago it was
-1.7 percent. As a contributor to employment, the manufacturing
sector is responsible for approximately 13.9 percent of total
employment in Barbados, 11.1 percent in Jamaica, and 19.6
percent in Trinidad and Tobago.

With the exception of Guyana, the manufacturing sector in
the Caribbean is primarily controlled by transnational corporations. Also, with the exception of Guyana, generous incentives
are provided for investment activities. Incentives to industrial
enterprises in the Caribbean include income tax holidays,
accelerated depreciation allowances and exemptions from import
duties, and subsidized rent for factory space. These incentives
reduce the cost of investment as part of the compensation for the
riskiness of new undertakings. From the point of view of the
government of Barbados, such incentives are intended to promote
investment in new ventures and the expansion of existing capacity
as well to generate new job opportunities. They are also used
to direct investment toward priority enterprises. [28]

Fiscal incentives have played a major role in the development
effort in the Caribbean and must be allowed to continue to do so
in the future. Because of fiscal incentives, transnational corporations have invested in the Caribbean. Such investment contributes
more than just financial resources. Managerial, administrative,
engineering, and other technical skills which are in short supply
in the Caribbean, are also provided. The petroleum-exporting and

the bauxite-mining industries, respectively, could not have been developed in Trinidad and Tobago and Guyana, for example, without assistance from transnational corporations. Moreover, transnational corporations investing through special fiscal concessions were responsible for the creation of 75 percent of the jobs in the manufacturing sector in Barbados and 44 and 20 percent respectively, in Trinidad and Tobago and Jamaica.[29] It would seem, therefore, that the employment created by transnational enterprises enjoying concessions in the manufacturing sector is extremely important to Barbados while it is of lesser importance to Jamaica and Trinidad and Tobago.

Investment by transnational corporations creates, directly and indirectly, employment opportunities. However, the extent of the employment opportunities created is determined by the nature of the investment. That is, whether the investment is more labour-intensive than capital-intensive or vice versa. For the Caribbean governments, the policy issue ought to be how to provide an environment in which private enterprise (both foreign and domestic) can contribute to national goals of employment creation while minimising the costs and maximising the benefits of such private investment. One aspect of providing such an environment and framework is for those Caribbean governments – Guyana in particular – that have acquired enterprises engaged in production or trade to consider divesting ownership in selected cases to increase yield and efficiency as well as provide a signal to investors of their interest in improving confidence in the private sector. Guyana's bauxite industry would be a prime candidate in this regard. Also, investors ought to be steered in such priority areas as petroleum exploration and fisheries development. Additionally, the Caribbean governments must be able to establish institutional frameworks through the various national banks and financial intermediaries to improve access to credit for small-scale industrial enterprises. This is most important since such enterprises are almost always labour-intensive and contribute to employment in a significant way. Moreover, because of the expanding seriousness of the unemployment crisis, it is not realistic for Caribbean governments to depend exclusively on medium- to large-scale firms to generate employment opportunities. Small-scale enterprises using appropriate technology that is not capital-intensive should therefore be encouraged.

Population Policies

Population policies in the Caribbean involve some cultural and institutional issues. These issues stem from the religious principles of certain segments of the population as well as the historical government positions *vis-à-vis* family planning. The view that lower fertility rates are desirable in the Caribbean is quite widespread[30] and family planning programs do play an important part in reducing fertility.   Moreover, such programs are less expensive, in terms of public investment, than urban and rural development programs.   Barbados, Jamaica, and Trinidad and Tobago have adopted family planning as a matter of national policy while the government of Guyana is yet to adopt an official policy.   Family planning is rooted in Barbados having been adopted by the government in 1967.   The official program operates largely through the Family Planning Association (an affiliate of the International Planned Parenthood Federation) and receives financial and other support from the government.   In Jamaica, family planning became part of government policy in 1966.   A National Family Planning Board was created in 1967 and, with the passage of the National Family Planning Act of 1970, was vested with full statutory responsibility for family planning programs.   In 1967 the government of Trinidad and Tobago adopted its family planning policy and family planning services are provided through the health system.

Lower fertility is not an end in itself, but one of among several ways of improving human welfare.   Population growth and family size can also be reduced by increased education and by basic health services which reduce infant mortality. In general, however, promoting family planning is the most widely accepted, practical, and cost-effective aspect of population policy. It goes without saying, therefore, that family planning programs must continue to be encouraged and supported at the governmental level in the Caribbean.   Moreover, the other Caribbean nations should follow Jamaica's lead and establish family planning programs that pay particular attention to the needs of teenagers as a direct response to the problem of adolescent pregnancy. Adolescent pregnancy is an acute problem in the Caribbean accounting for about one-third of all births, and in Jamaica, for example, more than 70 percent of the births are to unmarried mothers.

To deal with this problem the Jamaican Women's Bureau established, in January 1978, "The Women's Centre" to implement broadly based programs, that provide continuing education to pregnant teenagers and help them return to the school system, as creative strategies designed to reduce high fertility levels. The success of the Women's Centre in reducing high teenage fertility levels in Jamaica demonstrates that governmental concern coupled with a dedicated staff can provide positive results in the fight to lower fertility rates. [31] As the problem of adolescent pregnancy continues to grow in the Caribbean, the Women's Centre provides a significant example for other governments and agencies to follow.

Family planning necessarily entails the use of contraceptives. Without modern contraceptives, the costs of preventing pregnancy are much higher — sexual abstinence, withdrawal, abortion, infanticide. [32] Data from the World Fertility Survey (WFS) indicate that contraceptive awareness in the four countries in this study exceed 95 percent. That is, among currently married fecund women, more than 95 percent are aware of one or more efficient contraceptive methods. As with contraceptive awareness, contraceptive use in the Caribbean is also very high when comparison is made with other developing countries. Of a Latin America and Caribbean regional average of 44 percent, the percentage of currently married, fecund women using contraceptives is 35 percent in Guyana, 44 percent in Jamaica, and 56 percent in Trinidad and Tobago. Contraceptive use in the Caribbean is comparatively low among women under age 30 and rises substantially after that. This suggests that women in the Caribbean are more likely to adopt contraception when they have had all the children they want.[33] It also further explains the high rate of adolescent pregnancy in the Caribbean.

A primary issue for policy makers in the Caribbean, wanting to influence fertility trends, is the extent to which contraceptive use is affected by the availability of family planning services. Though the data is limited, it indicates that in Barbados and Trinidad and Tobago more than 90 percent of currently married women are aware of family planning outlets and sources of family planning supplies. The data also suggests that educational attainment and urbanization are critical ingredients in the mix of factors contributing to high contraceptive use. Contraceptive use increases dramatically as women's years of schooling rise. Likewise, as urbanization increases, contraceptive use increases and most of that can be attributed to the wider availability of contraceptives in urban areas.[34] All of this is consistent with the higher rates of fertility in the rural than in the urban areas and leads to the conclusion that efforts must be made to emphasize family planning in Caribbean rural communities although resistance is likely to be encountered for purely traditional reasons.

Before the 1960s, family planning services in the Caribbean were provided largely by voluntary associations. In the 1960s governmental commitment became pronounced. Such commitment must continue. Family planning services do help to lower fertility and have been shown to do so even among low-income groups. Caribbean governments must therefore intensify efforts to fund and promote family planning programs as a means to reducing population growth. Population policies in the Caribbean cannot, of course, be seen in isolation. Such policies must be integrated with the national health system as is the case in Trinidad and Tobago where the family planning unit exists within the Ministry of Health. In addition to administering such activities, the unit creates a climate within the health services conducive to the provision of family planning services as an integral part of the country's health care. Such a framework should be adopted by all Caribbean nations to enhance effectiveness and utilization particularly with respect to the rural population.

But whatever the form of integration and administration, a close interrelationship at the Ministerial level is essential for the success of family planning programs. Moreover, if targets are to be met then cooperation at the institutional level cannot be under-emphasized. Additionally, the gap between contraceptive use will be narrowed if such cooperative and integrative arrangements exist. Currently, this gap varies from a high of 60 percent in Guyana to a low of 39 percent in Trinidad and Tobago and is directly attributable to the lower use of contraceptives in the rural areas. Such integrated approaches must also extend the range of family planning services by building upon other development activities such as education, agricultural extension, cooperatives, women's organizations, and other rural-based economic and social programs.

Conclusions

If rural standards of living can be generally improved for the mass of the population then rural-urban migration can be checked. But the growth of the urban centers will not automatically stop. However, with an energetic movement away from strategies with an urban bias and a concentrated effort toward rural development, coupled with a firm population policy, urban population growth and urbanization in the Caribbean could become manageable.

Some of the policies advocated above exist in some facet in the Caribbean. That means, at least at the time of implementation, that they were deemed to be necessary and essential. The commitment and political support for these policies, and others discussed here, must be guaranteed if urban growth is to be stemmed. Such commitment and support is critical to any considerable success of these policies. In their absence these policies are doomed to failure. Political support cannot be taken for granted in the Caribbean. Decision-making there is highly centralized and urban-oriented and impacts negatively on the rural poor due to their political weakness. The political weakness of the rural poor can be reduced through human development programs that enhance their productive and organizational skills, their social status, and their command over information.[35] But even such programs are influenced by the political leadership in the Caribbean.

The problem with political support in the Third World, and the Caribbean is no exception, is that unless programs yield early political benefits to the politicians, continued political support cannot be taken for granted. Controlling and managing urban growth, however, will not occur overnight. It requires protracted policy endeavours, as suggested here, and some degree of patience.

Notes

1. Michael Lipton, *Why Poor People Stay Poor: Urban Bias in World Development* (Cambridge: Harvard University Press, 1977), p. 13.
2. *Ibid.*, p. 23.
3. See George Beckford, *Persistent Poverty: Underdevelopment in Plantation Economies of the Third World* (New York: Oxford University Press, 1972), p. 86; and P. Foster and P. Creyke, *The Structure of Plantation Agriculture in Jamaica* (College Park: University of Maryland, 1968), pp. 7-8.

4.   World Bank, *World Development Report 1979* (Washington, D.C.: World Bank, 1979), p. 59.

5.   See L.B. Coke and P.I. Gomes, "Critical Analysis of Agricultural Research and Development Institutions and their Activities", *Social and Economic Studies* 28 (March 1979), pp. 97-138.

6.   For a thorough discussion of the role of the GNCB in Guyana, see Kempe Ronald Hope, "National Cooperative Commercial Banking and Development Strategy in Guyana", *American Journal of Economics and Sociology* 34 (July 1975), pp. 309-322.

7.   See Kempe Ronald Hope, "Agriculture and Economic Development in the Caribbean", *Food Policy* 6 (November 1981), pp. 253-265.

8.   Gladstone Lewars, *Small Farm Financing in Guyana 1968-1970* (Kingston, Jamaica: Institute of Social and Economic Research, University of the West Indies, 1977), p. 74.

9.   David Wirmark, "Saving for Development", *Savings and Development* 7, No. 1 (1983), pp. 80-81.

10.   See Uma J. Lele, "The Role of Credit and Marketing Functions in Agricultural Development", A Paper Prepared for the International Economic Association Conference in Bad Godesberg, Germany, August 26 – September 4, 1972 , p. 1.

11.   World Bank, Agriculture and Rural Development Department, *Policy Paper on Agricultural Credit* (Washington, D.C.: World Bank, January 18, 1974), p. 29.

12.   For a greater elaboration of this idea, see Kempe Ronald Hope, "The Role of Savings in the Financing of Economic Development in the Caribbean," *Savings and Development* 6, No. 4 (1982), pp. 381-391; and Dale W. Adams, "Mobilizing Household Savings Through Rural Financial Markets," *Economic Development and Cultural Change* 26 (April 1978), pp. 547-560.

13.   See, for example, US Department of Agriculture, *Improving Marketing Systems in Developing Countries* (Washington, D.C.: US Department of Agriculture, Foreign Economic Development Service, February 1972), p. 28.

14.   For a good analysis of the beneficial impact of rural nonfarm activities, see, for example, Sunil Guha, "Income Redistribution Through Labour-Intensive Rural Public Works: Some Policy Issues", *International Labour Review* 120 (January-February 1981), pp. 67-82.

15.   See World Bank, *Rural Enterprise and Nonfarm Employment* (Washington, D.C.: World Bank, January 1978).

16.   Michael Lipton, *Why Poor People Stay Poor: Urban Bias in World Development*, pp. 334-336.

17.   A good review of this literature can be found in Norman T. Uphoff, John M. Cohen and Arthur A. Goldsmith, *Feasibility and Application of Rural Development Participation: A State-of-the-Art Paper* (Ithaca: Rural Development Committee, Cornell University, 1979).

18. International Labour Office, *Growth, Employment and Basic Needs in Latin America and the Caribbean* (Geneva: International Labour Office, 1979), p. 76.

19. See Kempe Ronald Hope, "Rural Development and Social Change", *Rural Development Digest* 3 (January 1980), pp. 1-7.

20. For a discussion of the issues pertaining to both the problems encountered and the benefits derived from such participation see, for example, Jerry Van Sant and Others, *Management Support to the Jamaican Ministry of Agriculture: Second Integrated Rural Development Project* (Washington, D.C.: Development Alternatives, Inc., April 1981); and Arthur Goldsmith and Harvey S. Blustain, *Local Organization and Participation in Integrated Rural Development in Jamaica* (Ithaca: Rural Development Committee, Cornell University, February 1980).

21. John D. Montgomery, "The Populist Front in Rural Development: Or Shall We Eliminate the Bureaucrats And Get On With the Job", *Public Administration Review* 39 (January-February 1979), p. 58.

22. Amilcar O. Herrera, "The Generation of Technologies in Rural Areas", *World Development* 9 (January 1981), p. 28.

23. Peter Hakim, "Lessons From Grass-Root Development Experience in Latin America and the Caribbean", *Assignment Children* 59/60, No. 2 (1982), p. 138.

24. See George Honadle and Others, *Implementing Capacity Building in Jamaica: Field Experience in Human Resource Development* (Washington, D.C.: Development Alternatives Inc., September 1980).

25. Harry W. Richardson, "National Urban Development Strategies in Developing Countries", *Urban Studies* 18 (October 1981), p. 279. See also Dennis A. Rondinelli, *Secondary Cities in Developing Countries* (Beverly Hills: Sage, 1983).

26. Dudley Seers, "The New Role of Development Planning" in B. Jalan (ed.) *Problems and Policies in Small Economies* (New York: St. Martin's Press, 1982), p. 78.

27. See Kempe Ronald Hope, "The Caribbean Tourism Sector: Recent Performance and Trends", *International Journal of Tourism Management* 1 (September 1980), pp. 175-183.

28. Winston Cox, "The Manufacturing Sector in the Economy of Barbados 1946-1980" in Delisle Worrell (ed.) *The Economy of Barbados 1946-1980* (Bridgetown, Barbados: Central Bank of Barbados, 1982), pp 48-49.

29. The figures for Barbados and Jamaica are derived from United Nations, "The Role of Fiscal Incentives for Employment Promotion in the Manufacturing Industries in Central America and Selected Caribbean Countries" in International Labour Office (eds.) *Fiscal Incentives for Employment Promotion in Developing Countries* (Geneva: International Labour Office, 1973), pp. 183-211. The figures for Trinidad and Tobago are derived from

Terisa Turner, *Multinational Enterprises and Employment in the Caribbean With Special Reference to Trinidad and Tobago* (Geneva: International Labour Office, Working Paper No. 20, 1982).

30. Sidney Chernick and Others, *The Commonwealth Caribbean: The Integration Experience* (Baltimore: Johns Hopkins University Press, 1978), 64-65.

31. The nature and success of the programs are well documented in Pamela McNeil and Others, "The Women's Centre in Jamaica: An Innovative Project for Adolescent Mothers", *Studies in Family Planning* 14 (May 1983), pp. 143-149.

32. Nancy Birdsall, "Population Growth and Poverty in the Developing World", *Population Bulletin* 35 (December 1980), p. 37.

33. Robert Lightbourne Jr., Susheela Singh, and Cynthia P. Green, "The World Fertility Survey: Charting Global Childbearing", *Population Bulletin* 37 (March 1982), p. 31.

34. *Ibid.,* pp. 37-40.

35. For more on this, see Norman Uphoff, "Political Considerations in Human Development" in Peter T. Knight (ed.) *Implementing Programs of Human Development* (Washington, D.C.: World Bank Staff Working Paper No. 403, July 1980), pp. 1-108.

5

SUMMARY AND CONCLUSIONS

The consequences of rapid urban population growth and concentrated urbanization in the Caribbean lead to diseconomies of scale and negative externalities. These in turn impact upon urban economic growth in a negative way and, ultimately, upon national economic growth also. This work has both argued for and advocated a set of policies necessary to make urbanization and urban population growth manageable in the Caribbean. In general terms, such policy formation is relatively straightforward. The real issue is one of government priorities and government decision-making on the allocation of scarce resources and, hence, the extent to which Caribbean governments would like to remove the urban bias that currently exists.

In the rural areas themselves there is no great mystery about what needs to be done. There has to be more efficient use of, and greater access to, basic resources of land, water and energy; expansion of non-farm employment through diversification of rural economies; improved supplies of agricultural inputs, credit and other services for small farmers; better education and health to improve the capacity of the rural population and thereby help in reducing the rate of population growth; more rapid expansion of infrastructure; and better organization of the rural population to mobilize themselves to give them greater bargaining power in the political process.[1]

But rural development does not nor cannot proceed in isolation in the Caribbean. It must be integrated in nature and be accompanied by other necessary urban development and popula-

101

tion policies. Rural development, however, has a critical role to play in minimizing unmanageable rural-urban migration especially since it is now increasingly apparent that migrants are no longer either the fuel for urban-industrial development or capable of being absorbed in "informal" activities. There is a growing predominance of rural-urban migration over other forms of migration and it is increasingly unidirectional (towards the primate city) and hence contributes to rapid urban growth and urban unemployment.[2] As such, the role of the primate city in the Caribbean is crucial in the development effort there. However, primate cities in the Caribbean have not been able to respond to the pressures that have resulted from rapid population increases while at the same time the concentration of resources in such cities have given rise to the current state of urban bias in Caribbean development policy. As such, the diffusion of urbanization through secondary city development becomes even more important.

Secondary city development can promote more equitable economic growth in the rural areas aside from whatever impact it has on slowing population growth and rapid urbanization in the urban areas. Developing secondary cities is one means of spreading the benefits of urbanization to larger numbers of people and of reducing interregional disparities. These benefits include commercialization of agriculture, provision of better services to residents in rural regions, national spatial integration, diffusion of social and technical innovations from the major metropolitan areas and from abroad, the decentralization of job opportunities, and, most important of all, the more equitable distribution of welfare (among urban areas and among regions) resulting from an intermediate city strategy.[3]

It is important to distinguish secondary city strategies from growth center strategies. The former are not primarily concerned with the attraction of large-scale industry to generate regional development. Instead, they focus much more on indigenous development which implies much more attention to measures that stimulate small-scale industry and the informal sector. Because secondary cities are also service centers for the surrounding rural hinterland, the strategy also implies attempts to strengthen urban-rural linkages through the development of agro-based industries and expansion in the production of agricultural inputs.[4] That is, the development of secondary cities as a way of creating more efficient agroprocessing and agricultural support industries in rural regions, providing greater access for rural people to both commercial and personal services, increasing food production, and providing off-farm employment opportunities.[5]

Also of related importance in the reasoning for developing secondary cities is the role they can play in the decentralization of the urban administration for national development. Administrative decentralization in the Caribbean is a long overdue policy reform and has been advocated on several occasions in the past.[6] Government offices and services have traditionally been located in the Caribbean urban areas, in the primate cities in particular, a practice which was both convenient and logical in the days of a more limited role for government. However, as Caribbean governments have taken a more activist role *vis-à-vis* national development, and as they have become involved in providing services for citizens as well as the need to involve more citizens in their programs, this physical concentration in the urban areas has become less practical. But, administrative decentralization has been resisted in the Caribbean primarily because of the reluctance of the various governments and their respective bureaucracies to cooperate in such efforts. Urban based staff are reluctant to leave the capital cities for the less developed rural areas; this in turn works against rural development which makes the rural areas still less developed and unattractive. Moreover, decentralization entails the erosion of the urban power base of the political elite.

Decentralization must be vigorously pursued in the Caribbean, however. Decentralization is conventionally defined as one of three things: (a) "deconcentration" — transferring resources and decision-making from headquarters to other branches of central government; (b) "devolution" — to autonomous units of government such as municipalities and local governments; and (c) "delegation" — to organizations outside the regular bureaucratic structure, such as public corporations and regional development authorities, or even to nongovernmental bodies such as farmer cooperatives, credit associations, and trade unions. Usually, in practice, the three forms are often combined with the most common form being deconcentration.[7] Decentralizing government activities in the Caribbean can result in a reduction in the need for coordination and increased efficiency in the delivery of services to both the urban and rural client population. Such physical and structural redistribution of functions and resources away from the existing organizational center must be the major thrust of administrative decentralization in the Caribbean. In more specific terms, this means establishing secondary offices to take services and responsibilities out of the primate cities and encouraging the delegation of functions both in the capital cities and in the secondary cities. The experience of Tunisia in the administration of its rural development programs would be most useful as a model in this regard.

It must be borne in mind, however, that decentralization is more an art than a science. As such, simply shifting decision-making authority away from the urban centers will not be sufficient to make decentralization a reality. The concentration of power and authority at the political level in the Caribbean does not allow for this. Expected outcomes depend therefore on the extent to which the various actors (politicians, bureaucrats, citizenry) perceive the differences in perspective among themselves and their respective capacities to confront and resolve them. The differences in perspective among these actors are organizational imperatives, not just personal differences, although their manifestations sometimes become heated as the issues affect daily operations. Channels can become almost sacred. Sharing knowledge about project experiences invites a sharing of decisions and disturbs the natural order of things as seen from the bureaucratic perspective. Sharing information, in short, is not always standard practice.[8] In the Caribbean it is not practised at all. This means that the factors that influence decentralization policy implementation have to be given adequate attention in the Caribbean. The compliance view of administration will not work there and, as such, the intended results of decentralization will not be achieved in a totally nonpolitical and technically competent way. Such is the current nature of politics and centralized authority in the Caribbean and it must be figured into the decentralization policy equation there, however disturbing and disrupting an influence it may be.

Undoubtedly, the issue of greatest importance arising from rapid urban population growth and urbanization in the Caribbean is that of urban unemployment. The rapid growth of the urban labour force in the Caribbean creates a supply of labour that, for policy purposes, is given when decisions are to be made concerning investment patterns, allocation of resources, planning, and so on. Since most of the labour force that will be active in the year 2000 has already been born, there is only one viable solution to the problem of dealing with such large numbers in the near future. That is, by assuring that the demand side of the labor market will absorb such a large quantity. Toward this end, however, there is little or no overall strategy for the very short-run which also guarantees a steady growth of jobs for the next twenty or thirty years and allows for economic expansion in all sectors. In other words, crash employment programs of a public works nature, as practised in the past in Jamaica will certainly help the immediate problem of creating jobs so that family income can be maintained. However, such programs, by their very nature, are usually beneficial only in the short-run — and if incomes are to be maintained beyond the life of those programs then other job opportunities must be available for the workers.

Whereas these short-run programs are necessary in the Caribbean there is a greater need to develop a long-range strategy to meet the challenges posed by the rapid increases in the urban labour force. The employment problem cannot be approached the same way within all sectors of the Caribbean, but it does seem clear that the approaches advocated in this work must be tried soon. Increasingly also, evidence is pointing to the need for alternate forms of technology to be applied to solve the problem of labour underutilization. Technologies which favour the use of labour can and must be applied in the Caribbean without sacrificing productivity. Moreover, it has been argued also that the challenge to technology for the Caribbean is the modernization of the region.[9] In the long-run these technologies will lead to a more viable development pattern since an important element will be to create jobs and hence increase income and spending power for a larger portion of the population.

Technology can be defined as the skills, knowledge, and procedures used in the provision of goods and services for any given society. Due to the unique features of the Caribbean economy, technology must be seen in the context of what is appropriate. The concept of appropriate technology must be looked at only in relation to some specified historical context and in terms of demand (basic needs goals) and supply (the appropriate production processes).[10] There is an urgent need for the harmonization of these two factors to bring about the management and production techniques that are best suited to the resources and future development potential of the Caribbean nations. Such technology must contribute not only to greater productive employment opportunities but also to the elimination of poverty and the achievement of an equitable distribution of income.

To this end industrialization policy looms large. For industrialization to be successful in the Caribbean, foreign investment will have to play a major role. The Caribbean needs foreign capital, know-how, and markets while foreign investors need security and a reasonable return on their investments. The very specifics of industrialization compel the Caribbean nations to provide a climate conducive to the encouragement of private foreign investment particularly that investment which is labour-intensive. Apart from providing employment, inflows of private investment can have a wide range of other potential impacts on host country development objectives.[11] They can affect the generation of income, foreign exchange, tax revenues and other areas at the macroeconomic level; affect regional and personal income distribution; change socio-economic values; and have dynamic effects on competition, industrial efficiency, technological development and product innovation.

Caribbean governments must enhance their investment incentive packages. Such investment incentives are a major factor in the investment decision of transnational corporations, particularly the tax concessions portion of it.[12] A country that does not grant tax incentives will be at a disadvantage in competing for private foreign investment since tax incentives significantly influence the composition of total investment.[13] Additionally, tax incentives are an efficient way to offset such disincentives as poor general economic policies and a lack of structural factors favourable to private investment as is the case in the Caribbean.

However, like rural and urban development, industrialization has to proceed simultaneously with agricultural development in the Caribbean. Industrial and agricultural development have too often been viewed as conflicting objectives. But agriculture provides the market for manufactured goods, satisfies the food requirements of the urban population, releases labour and capital for the industrial sector, and earns the foreign exchange required for the importation of machinery and raw materials. Industry in turn supplies the inputs required for modernization of the agricultural sector and the consumer goods demanded by the rural population, and provides a market for a part of the agricultural output through the processing and manufacture of foodstuffs for both domestic consumption and export. These are basically the arguments for "balanced growth" between the two sectors.[14] The concern for macrolevel development, industrialization, advanced technology, and transnational investment must be matched by concern and respect for agricultural development and, in the case of the Caribbean, particularly small farmer production and food-processing activities.

The links between agriculture and industry, and the mutual linkage effect of these two sectors are no longer in dispute *vis-à-vis* the Caribbean economies. The Caribbean economies have his-torically been agricultural in nature while at the same time existing side by side with a small highly capital-intensive non-agricultural sector. There also exists, in the agricultural sector itself, signifi-cant intrasectoral dualism. There are crops such as rice, sugar, and bananas which are grown primarily for export while at the same time there are more domestically oriented crops, like cassava, which are grown for local use. Because of the importance of agriculture (though declining in the past two decades) in the Caribbean economy, the way in which transfers are achieved from the agricultural to the industrial sector can determine the success, or the failure, of development efforts there. Unfortunately, the method used, knowingly or not, consists of modifying the terms of trade, to the detriment of the farmers, by keeping prices low for agricultural products and high for industrial goods. The effects of this method have generally been in the direction of dis-couraging agricultural production and consequently hindering industrial development. Given the disadvantages such artificial price modifications entail for farmers, Caribbean governments must try to compensate for them by subsidizing basic agricultural inputs, such as fertilizers, water, pesticides, and seeds. Caribbean farmers should not have to subsidize urban consumers through low food prices while at the same time paying high prices for urban manufactures.

Finally, some thoughts on population policies. In spite of the general effectiveness of family planning programs in the urban areas and the interest they have elicited, they have yet to be properly introduced and emphasized in the rural areas of the Caribbean. This is most important since there is considerable evidence proving the significance of economic and social conditions for the decrease in fertility. Moreover, there needs to be greater understanding of the links between direct population programs and other forms of intervention. These population programs not only need to be expanded, therefore, but should also be fully integrated in the socio-economic development plans of the various countries. Indeed, the other policy initiatives have little chance of success unless the brakes are put on population growth. Reducing the rate of population growth quickly could strain the social system in the Caribbean, but continuing on the current demographic trajectory will entail ruinous results. Further reductions in the fertility rate must be achieved while at the same time, however, the rates of infant mortality must be reduced.

The total number of children that a woman bears in her lifetime and the timing and spacing of her pregnancies have major impacts on each of her children's chances of survival. Indeed, among all the factors that influence infant mortality, fertility is one of the most important. But, unlike other factors, the relation between fertility and mortality is a two-way street. Low fertility tends to go together with low mortality as does high fertility and high mortality. Women who start childbearing while in their teens or prolong it past their mid-thirties increase the chance that their children will die in infancy.[15] Herein also lies the importance of family planning, particularly at the rural level. Most of the Caribbean's rural/urban differentials in mortality under the age of two years seem to originate in the different educational composition of both areas although some residual variation remains which could be attributable to other compositional contrasts or to an unequal allocation of resources between the rural and urban areas. The level of a mother's education seems to explain much of the variation in mortality levels within the population.[16] Since the necessary data are not available, it is difficult to say whether or not the importance of education reflects also associated factors such as income and occupation. However, it has been shown that the net effects of education, after controlling for other factors, remain important in explaining mortality differentials.[17] Progress in the area of mortality is never irreversible and efforts must continue to ensure that life expectancy both at birth and old ages is expanded.

From this study it is readily apparent that strong measures must be urgently taken to alleviate the doubly difficult situation of overcrowded urban centers and underdeveloped rural areas in the Caribbean. Common features of both are unemployment and underdevelopment and the economic forecast, both currently and in the long-run, is for marginal growth; high levels of inefficiency; and continued centralized economic decision-making. Without the implementation of viable programs, some of which are advocated in this work, then the situation will remain unmanageable.

Notes

1. M. Santa Cruz, "Reforming the Rural-Urban Contract", *Food Policy* 4 (May 1979), pp. 139-140.

2. See John Connell, "Rural Development: Green, White, Red or Blue Revolution" in John Friedmann, Ted Wheelwright, and John Connell (eds.) *Development Strategies in the Eighties* (Sydney: Development Studies Colloquium, University of Sydney, 1980), pp. 97-99.

3. Harry W. Richardson, *City Size and National Spatial Strategies in Developing Countries* (Washington, D.C.: World Bank Staff Working Paper No. 252, 1977), p. 17.

4. Harry W. Richardson, "National Urban Development Strategies in Developing Countries", *Urban Studies* 18 (October 1981), p. 279.

5. Dennis A. Rondinelli, *Secondary Cities in Developing Countries: Policies for Diffusing Urbanization* (Beverly Hills: Sage Publications, 1983), p. 36.

6. See, for example, Kempe Ronald Hope, "Development Administration in Post-Independence Guyana", *International Review of Administrative Sciences* 43, No. 1 (1977), pp. 67-72; and Kempe Ronald Hope, "The Administration of Development in Emergent Nations: The Problems in the Caribbean", *Public Administration and Development* 3 (January 1983), pp. 49-59.

7. World Bank, *World Development Report 1983* (New York: Oxford University Press, 1983), p. 120.

8. John D. Montgomery, "Decentralizing Integrated Rural Development Activities" in G. Shabbir Cheema and Dennis A. Rondinelli (eds.) *Decentralization and Development: Policy Implementation in Developing Countries* (Beverly Hills: Sage Publications, 1983), pp. 231-269.

9. J. Dellimore, "Intermediate Technology and the Modernization of Anglophone Caribbean States" in D.B. Thomas and M.S. Wionczek (eds.) *Integration of Science and Technology With Development: Caribbean and*

Latin American Problems in the Context of the United Nations Conference on Science and Technology for Development (New York: Pergamon Press, 1979), pp. 81-97.

10.   Kempe Ronald Hope, "The New International Economic Order, Basic Needs, and Technology Transfer: Toward an Integrated Strategy for Development in the Future", *World Futures* 18, Nos. 3 & 4 (1982), p. 169.

11.   See K. Billerbeck and Y. Yasugi, *Private Direct Foreign Investment in Developing Countries* (Washington, D.C.: World Bank Staff Working Paper No. 348, July 1979).

12.   Isaiah Frank, *Foreign Enterprise in Developing Countries* (Baltimore: Johns Hopkins University Press, 1980), pp. 95-96.

13.   David Lim, "Taxation Policies" in John Cody, Helen Hughes, and David Wall (eds.) *Policies for Industrial Progress in Developing Countries* (New York: Oxford University Press, 1980), pp. 175-185.

14.   David Colman and Frederick Nixson, *Economics of Change in Less Developed Countries* (New York: John Wiley and Sons, 1978), pp. 180-181.

15.   Kathleen Newland, *Infant Mortality and the Health of Societies* (Washington, D.C.: Worldwatch Papers, 1981), pp. 37-38.

16.   United Nations, *Levels and Trends of Mortality Since 1950* (New York: United Nations, 1982), p. 169.

17. *Ibid.*

SELECT BIBLIOGRAPHY

Abdulah, Norma. 1977. *The Labour Force in the Commonwealth Caribbean: A Statistical Analysis.* St. Augustine, Trinidad: Institute of Social and Economic Research, University of the West Indies.

Ainsworth, Martha. 1985. *Family Planning Programs: The Clients' Perspective.* Washington, D.C.: World Bank Staff Working Paper Numner 676.

Anderson, Dennis, and Mark W. Leiserson. 1980. "Rural Nonfarm Employment in Developing Countries". *Economic Development and Cultural Change,* Vol. 28, January, 227-248.

Anker, Richard, Mayra Buvinic, and Nadia Youseff (eds.) 1981. *Women's Roles and Population Trends in the Third World.* London: Croom Helm.

Anker, Richard, and Ghazi M. Farooq. 1978. "Population and Socio-Economic Development: The New Perspective". *International Labour Review,* Vol. 117, March-April, 143-155.

Arizpe, Lourdes. 1982. "Women and Development in Latin America and the Caribbean: Lessons From the Seventies and Hopes for the Future". *Development Dialogue,* Nos. 1 & 2, 74-84.

Ayub, Mahmood Ali. 1981. *Made in Jamaica: The Development of the Manufacturing Sector.* Baltimore: Johns Hopkins University Press.

Bailey, Wilma, and Dorian Powell. 1982. "Patterns of Contraceptive Use in Kingston and St. Andrew, Jamaica, 1970-1977". *Social Science and Medicine,* Vol. 16, No. 19, 1675-1683.

Bairoch, Paul. 1982. "Employment and Large Cities: Problems and Outlook". *International Labour Review,* Vol. 121, September-October, 519-533.

——————. 1975. *The Economic Development of the Third World Since 1900.* Berkeley: University of California Press.

——————. 1973. *Urban Unemployment in Developing Countries.* Geneva: International Labour Office.

Beckford, George. 1972. *Persistent Poverty: Underdevelopment in Plantation Economies of the Third World.* New York: Oxford University Press.

Bennell, Paul, and John Oxenham. 1983. "Skills and Qualifications for Small Island States". *Labour and Society,* Vol. 8, January-March, 13-37.

Berry, Albert, and R.H. Sabot. 1984. "Unemployment and Economic Development". *Economic Development and Cultural Change,* Vol. 33, October, 99-116.

Birdsall, Nancy. 1980. *Population and Poverty in the Developing World.* Washington, D.C.: World Bank Staff Working Paper No. 404.

Blair, Thomas L. 1983. "Third World Urban Innovation: Managing Growth and Development", *Cities,* Vol. 1, August, 71-84.

Blaug, Mark. 1974. *Education and the Employment Problem in Developing Countries.* Geneva: International Labour Office.

Boserup, Ester. 1970. *Women's Role in Economic Development.* New York: St. Martin's Press.

Bourne, Larry S. 1982. *Internal Structure of the City: Readings on Urban Form, Growth and Policy.* New York: Oxford University Press.

Bouvier, Leon F. 1983. *Barbados: Yesterday, Today and Tomorrow.* Washington, D.C.: Population Reference Bureau.

Braithwaite, Farley. 1983. *Unemployment and Social Life: A Sociological Study of the Unemployed in Trinidad.* Bridgetown, Barbados: Antilles Publications.

Brody, Eugene B. 1981. *Sex, Contraception, and Motherhood in Jamaica.* Cambridge: Harvard University Press.

Brown, Lester R. 1983. *Population Policies for a New Economic Era.* Washington, D.C.: Worldwatch Institute.

Brown, Lester R., and Pamela Shaw. 1982. *Six Steps to a Sustainable Society.* Washington, D.C.: Worldwatch Institute.

Brunn, Stanley D., and Jack F. Williams. 1983. *Cities of the World: World Regional Urban Development.* New York: Harper and Row.

Chambers, Robert. 1983. *Rural Development: Putting the Last First.* New York: Longman.

—————. 1974. *Managing Rural Development.* New York: Holmes and Meier.

Charlton, Sue Ellen M. 1984. *Women in Third World Development.* Boulder: Westview Press.

Cheema, G. Shabbir, and Dennis A. Rondinelli (eds.). 1983. *Decentralization and Development: Policy Implementation in Developing Countries.* Beverly Hills: Sage Publications.

Chernick, Sidney E. 1978. *The Commonwealth Caribbean: The Integration Experience.* Baltimore: Johns Hopkins University Press.

Clarke, Colin G. 1975. *Kingston, Jamaica: Urban Development and Social Change 1692-1962.* Berkeley: University of California Press.

Cochrane, Susan H. 1979. *Fertility and Education: What Do We Really Know?* Baltimore: Johns Hopkins University Press.

Cody, John, Helen Hughes, and David Wall (eds.). 1980. *Policies for Indus-*

trial Progress in Developing Countries. New York: Oxford University Press.

Cole, William E., and Richard D. Sanders. 1985. "Internal Migration and Urban Employment in the Third World". *American Economic Review,* Vol. 75, June, 481-494.

Connell, John, Biplab Dasgupta, Roy Laishley, and Michael Lipton. 1976. *Migration from Rural Areas: The Evidence From Village Studies.* Delhi: Oxford University Press.

Coombs, Philip, and Manzoor Ahmed. 1974. *Attacking Rural Poverty: How Nonformal Education Can Help.* Baltimore: Johns Hopkins University Press.

Cox, Winston. 1982. "The Manufacturing Sector in the Economy of Barbados 1946-1980". In *The Economy of Barbados 1946-1980.* Edited by De Lisle Worrell. Bridgetown, Barbados: Central Bank of Barbados.

Cross, Malcolm. 1979. *Urbanization and Urban Growth in the Caribbean: An Essay on Social Change in Dependent Societies.* New York: Cambridge University Press.

Cuca, Roberto. 1979. *Family Planning Programs: An Evaluation of Experience.* Washington, D.C.: World Bank Staff Working Paper No. 345.

Davies, Omar. 1984. "Housing: The Basis for a National Policy in Jamaica". Occasional Papers, No. 3, Economics Department, University of the West Indies.

De Albuquerque, Klaus, Wesley Van Riel, and Mark J. Taylor. 1980. "Uncontrolled Urbanization in the Developing World: A Jamaican Case Study". *Journal of Developing Areas,* Vol. 14, April, 361-386.

De Janvry, Alain. 1981. "The Role of Land Reform in Economic Development: Policies and Politics". *American Journal of Agricultural Economics,* Vol. 63, No. 2, 384-392.

Denton, E. Hazel. 1979. "Economic Determinants of Fertility in Jamaica". *Population Studies,* Vol. 33, July, 295-305.

Dovring, Folke. 1970. *Economic Results of Land Reform.* Washington, D.C.: U.S. Agency for International Development.

Dwyer, D.J. 1975. *People and Housing in Third World Cities.* London: Longman.

Edwards, Edgar O. (ed.). 1974. *Employment in Developing Nations.* New York: Columbia University Press.

Eyre, Alan. 1972. "The Shantytowns of Montego Bay, Jamaica". *Geographical Review,* Vol. 62, July, 394-413.

Farooq, Ghazi M. 1985. *Population and Employment in Developing Countries.* Geneva: International Labour Office.

Farrell, Trevor. 1978. "The Unemployment Crisis in Trinidad and Tobago: Its Current Dimensions and Some Projections to 1985". *Social and Economic Studies,* Vol. 27, June, 117-152.

Files, Laurel A. 1982. "A Re-examination of Integrated Population Activities". *Studies in Family Planning,* Vol. 13, October, 297-302.

Findley, Sally. 1977. *Planning for Internal Migration: A Review of Issues and Policies in Developing Countries.* Washington, D.C.: U.S. Government Printing Office.

Frejka, Tomas. 1981. *Population Dynamics and Prospects: A 1981 Assessment for Jamaica.* New York: Population Council, Working Paper No. 74.

Freidmann, John, and Flora Sullivan. 1974. "The Absorption of Labour in the Urban Economy: The Case of Developing Countries". *Economic Development and Cultural Change,* Vol. 22, April, 385-413.

Friedmann, John, and R. Wulff. 1976. *The Urban Tradition: Comparative Studies of Newly Industrializing Societies.* London: Edward Arnold.

Guade, Jacques, and Peter Peek. 1976. "The Economic Effects of Rural-Urban Migration". *International Labour Review,* Vol. 114, November-December, 329-337.

Ghai, Dharam, Eddy Lee, Justin Maeda, and Samir Radwan. 1979. *Overcoming Rural Underdevelopment.* Geneva: International Labour Office.

Gilbert, Alan, and Josef Gugler. 1982. *Cities, Poverty, and Development: Urbanization in the Third World.* New York: Oxford University Press.

Goldscheider, Calvin. 1983. "The Adjustment of Migrants in Large Cities of Less Developed Countries: Some Comparative Observations". In *Urban Migrants in Developing Nations: Patterns and Problems of Adjustment.* Edited by Calvin Goldscheider. Boulder: Westview Press.

Goldsmith, Arthur A., and Harvey S. Blustain. 1980. *Local Organization and Participation in Integrated Rural Development in Jamaica.* Ithaca: Rural Development Committee, Cornell University.

Goldstein, Sidney. 1983. "Urbanization, Migration, and Development". In *Urban Migrants in Developing Nations: Patterns and Problems of Adjustment.* Edited by Calvin Goldscheider. Boulder: Westview Press.

_____. 1979. *Migration and Rural Development.* Rome Food and Agriculture Organization, Economic and Social Development Paper No. 8.

Goldstein, Sidney, and Alice Goldstein. 1981. *Surveys of Migration in Developing Countries: A Methodological Review.* Honolulu: East-West Population Institute, Paper No. 71.

Government of Jamaica, National Planning Agency. 1978. *Urban Growth and Management Study: Final Report.* Kingston, Jamaica: National Planning Agency.

_____. 1978. *Urban Growth and Management Study: Interim Report No. 3.* Kingston, Jamaica: National Planning Agency.

Graham, Norman A., and Keith L. Edwards. 1984. *The Caribbean Basin to the Year 2000.* Boulder: Westview Press.

Grimes, Orville F., Jr. 1976. *Housing for Low-Income Urban Families.*

Baltimore: Johns Hopkins University Press.

Gugler, Josef. 1982. "Overurbanization Reconsidered". *Economic Development and Cultural Change,* Vol. 31, October, 173-189.

Guha, Sunil. 1981. "Income Redistribution Through Labour-Intensive Rural Public Works: Some Policy Issues". *International Labour Review,* Vol. 120, January-February, 67-82.

Hakim, Peter, 1982. "Lessons from Grass-Root Development in Latin America and the Caribbean". *Assignment Children,* Vol. 59/60, No. 2, 137-141.

Harewood, Jack. 1978. *Unemployment and Related Problems in the Commonwealth Caribbean.* St. Augustine, Trinidad: Institute of Social and Economic Research, University of the West Indies.

Harvey, Charles, Jake Jacobs, Geoff Lamb, and Bernard Schaffer. 1979. *Rural Employment and Administration in the Third World: Development Methods and Alternative Strategies.* Geneva: ILO/Saxon House.

Hauser, Philip M. 1979. "Introduction and Overview". In *World Population and Development.* Edited by Philip M. Hauser. Syracuse: Syracuse University Press.

Hope, Kempe Ronald. 1986. *Economic Development in the Commonwealth Caribbean: Essays on Growth and Change.* New York: Praeger Publishers.

_____. 1986. "Urbanization and Economic Development in the Third World". *Cities,* Vol. 3, February.

_____. 1985. *Internal Migration and Urbanization in the Caribbean.* Prepared for the Development Cooperation Secretariat, Organization of American States, Washington, D.C.

_____. 1985. "Urban Population Growth and Urbanization in the Caribbean". *Inter-American Economic Affairs,* Vol. 39, Summer, 31-49.

_____. 1984. *The Dynamics of Development and Development Administration.* Westport, Connecticut: Greenwood Press.

_____. 1984. "Unemployment, Labour Force Participation, and Urbanization in the Caribbean". *Review of Regional Studies,* Vol. 14, Fall, 9-16.

_____. 1983. "Urban Population Growth in the Caribbean". *Cities,* Vol. 1, November, 167-174.

_____. 1983. "Urban Development and Social Change: A Conceptual Analysis of an American Dilemma". *Habitat International,* Vol. 7, Nos. 3/4, 31-36.

_____. 1983. "Self-Reliance and Participation of the Poor in the Development Process in the Third World". *Futures,* Vol. 15, December, 455-462.

_____. 1983. "A Note on the Unemployment Problem in the Caribbean". *Labour and Society,* Vol. 8, July-September, 271-276.

_____. 1982. "Agriculture and the Urbanization Process in the Caribbean". In *Regional Development in Small Island Nations.* Edited by

Benjamin Higgins. Nagoya, Japan: United Nations Centre for Regional Development, Special Issue of *Regional Development Dialogue,* 65-78.

——————. 1982. "The Employment Problem, Rural-Urban Migration and Urbanization in the Caribbean". *Population Review,* Vol. 26, Nos. 1 & 2 40-54.

——————. 1981. "Agriculture and Economic Development in the Caribbean". *Food Policy,* Vol. 6, November, 253-265.

——————. 1980. "Rural Development and Social Change". *Rural Development Digest,* Vol. 3, January, 1-7.

——————. 1980. "The Caribbean Tourism Sector: Recent Performance and Trends". *International Journal of Tourism Management,* Vol. 1, September, 175-183.

——————. 1980. "Population, Labour and Employment in Caribbean Socio-Economic Development". In *Caribbean Issues of Emergence: Socio-Economic and Political Perspectives.* Edited by Vincent McDonald. Washington, D.C.: University Press of America.

——————. 1980. *Recent Performance and Trends in the Caribbean Economy: A Study of Selected Caribbean Countries.* St. Augustine, Trinidad: Institute of Social and Economic Research, University of the West Indies.

——————. 1978. "Strengthening Rural Cooperatives in Guyana". *Journal of Rural Cooperation,* Vol. 6, No. 2, 157-166.

——————. 1976. "The Emigration of High-Level Manpower from Developing to Developed Countries With Reference to Trinidad and Tobago". *International Migration,* Vol. 14, No. 3, 209-218.

——————. 1975. "Regional Community Development Planning in Guyana". *Social and Economic Studies,* Vol. 24, December, 504-508.

Hope, Kempe Ronald, and Terry Ruefli. 1981. "Rural-Urban Migration and the Development Process: A Caribbean Case Study". *Labour and Society,* Vol. 6, April-June, 141-148.

Inter-American Development Bank. 1983. *Economic and Social Progress in Latin America 1983.* Washington, D.C.: Inter-American Development Bank.

——————. 1979. *Economic and Social Progress in Latin America 1979.* Washington, D.C.: Inter-American Development Bank.

International Labour Office. 1979. *Growth, Employment and Basic Needs in Latin America and the Caribbean.* Geneva: International Labour Office.

——————. 1973. *Fiscal Incentives for Employment Promotion in Developing Countries.* Geneva: International Labour Office.

Jacobsen, Judith. 1983. *Promoting Population Stabilization: Incentives for Small Families.* Washington, D.C.: Worldwatch Institute.

Jagdeo, Tirbani P. 1984. *Teenage Pregnancy in the Caribbean.* New York: International Planned Parenthood Federation.

Jalan, B. (ed.). 1982. *Problems and Policies in Small Economies*. New York: St. Martin's Press.

Jones, H.R. 1977. "Metropolitan Dominance and Family Planning in Barbados". *Social and Economic Studies*, Vol. 26, September, 327-338.

Kanagaratnam, K., and C.S. Pierce. 1980. *Population Policy and Family Planning Programs: Trends in Policy and Administration*. Washington, D.C.: World Bank Staff Working Paper No. 411.

Kannappan, Subbiah, 1983. *Employment Problems and the Urban Labor Market in Developing Nations*. Ann Arbor: Graduate School of Business Administration, Division of Research, University of Michigan.

Kelly, Allen, C., and Jeffrey G. Williamson. 1982. "The Limits to Urban Growth: Suggestions for Macromodelling Third World Economies". *Economic Development and Cultural Change*, Vol. 30, April, 595-623.

Keyfitz, Nathan. 1978. "Do Cities Grow by Natural Increase or by Migration?" *Geographical Analysis*, Vol. 12, No. 2, 142-156.

Lapham, Robert J., and W. Parker Mauldin. 1984. "Family Planning Program Effort and Birthrate Decline in Developing Countries". *International Family Planning Perspectives*, Vol. 10, December, 109-118.

Ledent, Jacques. 1982. "Rural-Urban Migration, Urbanization, and Economic Development". *Economic Development and Cultural Change*, Vol. 30, April, 507-538.

Levy, John M. 1981. *Economic Development Programs for Cities, Counties, and Towns*. New York: Praeger Publishers.

Lewis, W. Arthur. 1978. *The Evolution of the International Economic Order*. Princeton: Princeton University Press.

Lightbourne, R.E., and Susheela Singh. 1982. "Fertility, Union Status and Partners in the WFS Guyana and Jamaica Surveys, 1975-1976". *Population Studies*, Vol. 36, July, 201-225.

Lightbourne, Robert, Jr., Susheela Singh, and Cynthia P. Green. 1982. "The World Fetility Survey: Charting Global Childbearing". *Population Bulletin*, Vol. 37, March, 1-54.

Linn, Johannes F. 1983. *Cities in the Developing World: Policies for their Equitable and Efficient Growth*. New York: Oxford University Press .

——————. 1982. "The Costs of Urbanization in Developing Countries". *Economic Development and Cultural Change*, Vol. 30, April, 625-648.

Lipton, Michael. 1977. *Why Poor People Stay Poor: Urban Bias in World Development*. Cambridge: Harvard University Press.

Londsdale, Richard E., and György Enyedi. (eds.). 1984. *Rural Public Services: International Comparisons*. Boulder: Westview Press.

Long, Frank. 1982. "The Food Crisis in the Caribbean". *Third World Quarterly*, Vol. 4, October, 758-770.

Loup, Jacques. 1983. *Can the Third World Survive?* Baltimore: Johns Hopkins University Press.

McAuslan, Patrick. 1985. *Urban Land and Shelter for the Poor*. Washington, D.C.: International Institute for Environment and Development.

McGreevey, William Paul. 1980. *Third World Poverty*. Lexington: Lexington Books.

McNeil, Pamela, Freya Olafson, Dorian L. Powell, and Jean Jackson. 1983. "The Women's Centre in Jamaica: An Innovative Project for Adolescent Mothers". *Studies in Family Planning*, Vol. 14, May, 143-149.

McNicoll, Geoffrey. 1984. "Consequences of Rapid Population Growth: Overview and Assessment". *Population and Development Review*, Vol. 10, June, 177-240.

Macon, Jorge, and Jose Merino Manon. 1977. *Financing Urban and Rural Development Through Betterment Levies*. New York: Praeger.

Marks, Arnaud F., and Hebe M.C. Vessuri (eds.). 1983. *White Collar Migrants in the Americas and the Caribbean*. Leiden, Netherlands: Department of Caribbean Studies, Royal Institute of Linguistics and Anthropology.

Massiah, Joycelin. 1983. *Women as Heads of Households in the Caribbean: Family Structure and Feminine Status*. Paris: UNESCO.

Mazumdar, Dipak. 1976. "The Urban Informal Sector". *World Development*, Vol. 4, August, 655-679.

———. 1975. "The Rural-Urban Wage Gap, Migration, and the Shadow Wage". *Oxford Economic Papers*, Vol. 28, November, 406-425.

Meier, Gerald M. 1984. *Emerging From Poverty: The Economics That Really Matters*. New York: Oxford University Press.

Miro, Carmen A., and Joseph E. Potter. 1980. *Population Policy: Research Priorities in the Developing World*. New York: St. Martin's Press.

Montgomery, John D. 1982. "Decentralizing Integrated Rural Development Activities". In *Decentralization and Development: Policy Implementation in Developing Countries*. Edited by G. Shabbir Cheema and Dennis A. Rondinelli. Beverly Hills: Sage Publications.

———. 1979. "The Populist Front in Rural Development: Or Shall We Eliminate the Bureaucrats And Get On With The Job?". *Public Administration Review*, Vol. 39, January-February, 58-65.

Murdoch, William W. 1980. *The Poverty of Nations*. Baltimore: Johns Hopkins University Press.

Nelson, Joan. 1979. *Access to Power: Politics and the Urban Poor in Developing Nations*. Princeton: Princeton University Press.

———. 1976. "Sojourners Versus New Urbanites: Causes and Consequences of Temporary Versus Permanent Cityward Migration in Developing Countries". *Economic Development and Cultural Change*, Vol. 24, July, 721-757.

———. 1970. "The Urban Poor: Disruption or Political Integration in Third World Cities?" *World Politics*, Vol. 22, April, 393-414.

Newland, Kathleen. 1981. *Infant Mortality and the Health of Societies*. Washington, D.C.: Worldwatch Institute.

—————. 1980. *City Limits: Emerging Constraints on Urban Growth.* Washington, D.C.: Worldwatch Institute.

Nyerere, Julius K. 1979. *On Rural Development.* Address to the Food and Agriculture Organization World Conference on Agrarian Reform and Rural Development, Rome, Italy, July 13.

Oakley, Peter and David Marsden. 1984. *Approaches to Participation in Rural Development.* Geneva: International Labour Office.

Oberai, A.S. 1978. *Changes in the Structure of Employment With Economic Development.* Geneva: International Labour Office.

—————. 1977. "Migration, Unemployment and the Urban Labour Market". *International Labour Review,* Vol. 115, March-April, 211-223.

Oeschli, Frank William, and Dudley Kirk. 1975. "Modernization and the Demographic Transition in Latin America and the Caribbean". *Economic Development and Cultural Change,* Vol. 23, April, 391-419.

Pacione, M. (ed.). 1981. *Problems and Planning in Third World Cities.* New York: St. Martin's Press.

Patterson, Orlando. 1978. "Migration in Caribbean Societies: Socioeconomic and Symbolic Resource". In *Human Migration: Patterns and Policies.* Edited by W.H. McNeill and R.S. Adams. Bloomington: Indiana University Press.

Payne, Geoffrey K. 1977. *Urban Housing in the Third World.* Boston: Routledge and Kegan Paul.

Peek, Peter, and Guy Standing. 1979. "Rural-Urban Migration and Government Policies in Low-Income Countries". *International Labour Review,* Vol. 118, November-December, 747-762.

Potter, Robert. 1985. *Urbanization and Planning in the Third World: Spatial Perceptions and Public Participation.* New York: St. Martin's Press.

Powell, Dorian. 1984. "The Role of Women in the Caribbean" *Social and Economic Studies,* Vol. 33, June, 97-122.

—————. 1976. "Female Labour Force Participation and Fertility: An Exploratory Study of Jamaican Women". *Social and Economic Studies,* Vol. 25, September, 234-258.

Preston, Samuel H. 1979. "Urban Growth in Developing Countries: A Demographic Reappraisal". *Population and Development Review,* Vol. 5, June, 195-216.

Quadeer, Mohammed A. 1983. *Urban Development in the Third World: Internal Dynamics of Lahore, Pakistan.* New York: Praeger.

Rao, D.C. 1974. "Urban Target Groups". In *Redistribution With Growth.* Edited by Hollis Chenery and Others. New York: Oxford University Press.

Renaud, Bertrand. 1981. *National Urbanization Policy in Developing Countries.* New York: Oxford University Press.

Rhoda, Richard. 1983. "Rural Development and Urban Migration: Can We Keep Them Down on the Farm?" *International Migration Review,* Vol. 17, Spring, 34-64.

Richardson, Harry W. 1981. "National Urban Development Strategies in Developing Countries". *Urban Studies,* Vol. 18, October, 267-283.

—————. 1977. *City Size and National Spatial Strategies in Developing Countries.* Washington, D.C.: World Bank Staff Working Paper No. 252.

Roberts, Bryan. 1978. *Cities of Peasants: The Political Economy of Urbanization in the Third World.* Beverly Hills: Sage Publications.

Roberts, George W. (ed.). 1974. *Recent Population Movements in Jamaica.* Kingston, Jamaica: CICRED.

Rodgers, Gerry. 1984. *Poverty and Population: Approaches and Evidence.* Geneva: International Labour Office.

—————. 1983. "The Impact of Rural-Urban Migration on Income Distribution". *Canadian Journal of Development Studies,* Vol. 4, No. 2, 275-296.

Rogers, Andrei. 1982. "Sources of Urban Population Growth and Urbanization 1950-200: A Demographic Accounting". *Economic Development and Cultural Change,* Vol. 30, April, 483-506.

Rogers, Andrei, and Jeffrey G. Williamson. 1982. "Migration, Urbanization, and Third World Development: An Overview". *Economic Development and Cultural Change,* Vol. 30, April, 463-482.

Rondinelli, Dennis A. 1985. *Applied Methods of Regional Analysis: The Spatial Dimensions of Development Policy.* Boulder: Westview Press.

—————. 1985. "Population Distribution and Economic Development in Africa: The Need for Urbanization Policies". *Population Research and Policy Review,* Vol. 4, June, 173-196.

—————. 1983. *Secondary Cities in Developing Countries: Policies for Diffusing Urbanization.* Beverly Hills: Sage Publications.

—————. 1983. "Towns and Small Cities in Developing Countries". *Geographical Review,* Vol. 73, October, 379-395.

Rondinelli, Dennis A., and Kenneth Ruddle. 1978. *Urbanization and Rural Development: A Spatial Policy for Equitable Growth.* New York: Praeger Publishers.

Ruddle, Kenneth, and Dennis A. Rondinelli. 1979. "Urban Functions in Rural Development: Integrating Spatial Systems for Equitable Growth". *Journal of Economic Development,* Vol. 4, July, 91-116.

Sabot, R.H. 1977. "The Meaning and Measurement of Urban Surplus Labour". *Oxford Economic Papers,* Vol. 29, November, 389-411.

Safa, Helen I. 1982. "Introduction". In *Towards a Political Economy of Urbanization in Third World Countries.* Edited by Helen I. Safa. New Delhi: Oxford University Press.

Scott, Hilda. 1984. *Working Your Way to the Bottom: The Feminization of Poverty.* London: Routledge and Kegan Paul.

Senderowitz, Judith, and John M. Paxman. 1985. "Adolescent Fertility: Worldwide Concerns". *Population Bulletin,* Vol. 40, April, 1-50.

Sethuraman, S.V. (ed.). 1981. *The Urban Informal Sector in Developing Countries.* Geneva: International Labour Office.

Simpson, Joy M. 1973. *Internal Migration in Trinidad and Tobago.* Kingston, Jamaica: Institute of Social and Economic Research, University of the West Indies.

Sinclair, Stuart W. 1978. *Urbanization and Labor Markets in Developing Countries.* New York: St. Martin's Press.

Singh, Ram D. 1977. "Labour Migration and its Impact on Employment and Income in a Small Farm Economy". *International Labour Review,* Vol. 116, November-December, 331-341.

Sivard, Ruth Legar. 1985. *Women: A World Survey* Washington, D.C.: World Priorities.

Speare, Alden. 1983. "Methodological Issues in the Study of Migrant Adjustment". In *Urban Migrants in Developing Nations: Patterns and Problems of Adjustment.* Edited by Calvin Goldscheider. Boulder: Westview Press.

Squire, Lyn. 1981. *Employment Policy in Developing Countries: A Survey of Issues and Evidence.* New York: Oxford University Press.

Stamper, B. Maxwell. 1977. *Population and Planning in Developing Nations.* New York: The Population Council.

Standing, Guy. 1982. "Contrived Stagnation, Migration and the State in Guyana". In *State Policies and Migration: Studies in Latin America and the Caribbean.* Edited by Peter Peek and Guy Standing. London: Croom Helm.

——————. 1981. *Unemployment and Female Labor: A Study of Labor Supply in Kingston, Jamaica.* New York: St. Martin's Press.

——————. 1978. *Migration, Labour Force Absorption and Mobility: Women in Kingston, Jamaica.* Geneva: International Labour Office, Population and Employment Working Paper No. 68.

——————. 1978. *Labour Force Participation and Development.* Geneva: International Labour Office.

——————. 1978. "Aspiration Wages, Migration and Urban Umemployment". *Journal of Development Studies,* Vol. 14, January, 232-248.

Standing, Guy, and Fred Sukdeo. 1977. "Labour Migration and Development in Guyana". *International Labour Review,* Vol. 116, November-December, 303-313.

Stark, Oded, and David Levhari. 1982. "On Migration and Risk in LDC's". *Economic Development and Cultural Change,* Vol. 31, October, 191-196.

Stockwell, Edward Grant, and Karen Anne Laidlaw. 1981. *Third World Development: Problems and Prespects.* Chicago: Nelson-Hall.

Stokes, Bruce. 1977. *Filling the Family Planning Gap.* Washington, D.C.: Worldwatch Institute.

Stretton, Hugh. 1978. *Urban Planning in Rich and Poor Countries.* New York: Oxford University Press.

Tidrick, G.M. 1975. "Wage Spillover and Unemployment in a Wage-Gap Economy: The Jamaican Case". *Economic Development and Cultural Change,* Vol. 23, January, 306-324.

Tilly, L.A., and J.W. Scott. 1978. *Women, Work and Family.* New York: Holt, Rinehart and Winston.

Todaro, Michael P. 1981. *City Bias and Rural Neglect: The Dilemma of Urban Development.* New York: Population Council.

————. 1980. "Urbanization in Developing Nations: Trends, Prospects, and Policies". *Journal of Geography,* Vol. 79, September/October, 164-174.

————. 1980. "Internal Migration, Urban Population Growth and Unemployment in Developing Nations: Issues and Controversies". *Journal of Economic Development,* Vol. 5, July, 7-23.

————. 1976. *Internal Migration in Developing Countries.* Geneva: International Labour Office.

Turner, Terisa. 1982. *Multinational Enterprises and Employment in the Caribbean With Special Reference to Trinidad and Tobago.* Geneva: International Labour Office.

Turnham, David, and I. Jaeger. 1971. *The Employment Problem in Less Developed Countries: A Review of the Evidence.* Paris: Organization for Economic Cooperation and Development.

United Nations, 1982. *Levels and Trends of Mortality Since 1950.* New York: United Nations.

————. 1981. *Population Distribution Policies in Development Planning.* New York: United Nations.

————. 1981. *World Population Prospects as Assessed in 1980.* New York: United Nations.

————. 1980. *Patterns of Urban and Rural Population Growth.* New York: United Nations.

————. 1974. *Urban-Rural Projections for 1950 to 2000.* New York: United Nations, Population Division.

————. 1973. *The Determinants and Consequences of Population Trends.* New York: United Nations.

————. 1970. *Administrative Aspects of Urbanization.* New York: United Nations.

Vu, My T. 1984. *World Population Projections 1984.* Washington, D.C.: World Bank.

Warriner, Doreen. 1969. *Land Reform in Principle and Practice.* London: Clarendon Press.

Wertheim, William F., and Matthias Stiefel. 1982. *Production, Equality and Participation in Rural China.* Geneva: United Nations Research Institute for Social Development.

Wheaton, William C., and Hisanobu Shishido. 1981. "Urban Contracentration, Agglomeration Economies, and the Level of Economic Development". *Economic Development and Cultural Change,* Vol. 30, October, 17-30.

Williams, Martin, and Mark Ondera. 1982. "Public Expenditures on Housing in Less Developed Countries". *Journal of Economic Development,* Vol. 7, July, 127-133.

World Bank. 1984. *World Development Report 1984.* New York: Oxford University Press.

—————. 1983. *World Development Report 1983.* New York: Oxford University Press.

—————. 1982. *World Development Report 1982.* New York: Oxford University Press.

—————. 1981. *World Development Report 1981.* New York: Oxford University Press.

—————. 1980. *World Development Report 1980.* Washington, D.C.: World Bank.

—————. 1979. *World Development Report 1979.* Washington, D.C.: World Bank.

—————. 1978. *World Development Report 1978.* Washington, D.C.: World Bank.

—————. 1978. *Rural Enterprise and Nonfarm Employment.* Washington, D.C.: World Bank.

—————. 1972. *Urbanization.* Washington, D.C.: World Bank, Sector Working Paper.

Yap, Lorene Y.L. 1977. "The Attraction of Cities: A Review of the Migration Literature". *Journal of Development Economics,* Vol. 4, September, 239-264.

Yinger, Nancy, Richard Osburn, David Salkever, and Ismail Sirageldin. 1983. "Third World Family Planning Programs: Measuring the Costs". *Population Bulletin,* Vol. 38, February, 1-35.

Youssef, Nadia, Mayra Buvinic, Ayse Kudat, Jennefer Sebstad, and Barbara Von Elm. 1979. *Women in Migration: A Third World Focus.* Washington, D.C.: International Center for Research on Women.

INDEX